《多彩中国节》丛书编委会
Editorial Committee of the Colorful Chinese Festivals Series

顾 问
史蒂文·伍德·施迈德　冯骥才　周明甫

主 编
彭新良

编 委（按姓名笔画排列）
韦荣慧　田　阡　邢　莉　刘　哲
齐勇锋　阮全友　张　刚　张　跃
张　暖　张曙光　陈　娟　徐　敏
黄忠彩　萧　放　曹雅欣　彭新良

Consultants

Steven Wood Schmader　Feng Jicai　Zhou Mingfu

Chief Editor

Peng Xinliang

Editorial Board

Wei Ronghui　Tian Qian　Xing Li　Liu Zhe

Qi Yongfeng　Ruan Quanyou　Zhang Gang　Zhang Yue

Zhang Nuan　Zhang Shuguang　Chen Juan　Xu Min

Huang Zhongcai　Xiao Fang　Cao Yaxin　Peng Xinliang

丛书主编　彭新良

The Lantern Festival

汉英对照

元宵节

张跃　王晓艳　等　编著
赵波　段佳燕　译

全国百佳图书出版单位
APTIME
时代出版
时代出版传媒股份有限公司
安徽人民出版社

图书在版编目（CIP）数据

元宵节：汉英对照 / 张跃，王晓艳等编著；赵波，段佳燕译 . -- 合肥：安徽人民出版社，2018.8
（多彩中国节丛书 / 彭新良主编）

ISBN 978-7-212-10024-7

Ⅰ . ①元… Ⅱ . ①张… ②王… ③赵… ④段… Ⅲ . ①节日—风俗习惯—中国—汉、英 Ⅳ . ① K892.1

中国版本图书馆 CIP 数据核字 (2018) 第 005204 号

《多彩中国节》丛书

元宵节：汉英对照
YUANXIAO JIE

彭新良　丛书主编
张跃　王晓艳　等　编著　　赵波　段佳燕　译

出 版 人：徐　敏		选题策划：刘　哲　陈　娟	
出版统筹：张　旻　袁小燕		责任编辑：王光生	
责任印制：董　亮		装帧设计：陈　爽　宋文岚	

出版发行　时代出版传媒股份有限公司 http://www.press-mart.com
　　　　　安徽人民出版社 http://www.ahpeople.com
地　　址　合肥市政务文化新区翡翠路 1118 号出版传媒广场八楼
邮　　编　230071
电　　话　0551-63533258　0551-63533259（传真）
印　　刷　安徽联众印刷有限公司

开本：880mm×1230mm　1/32　　印张：8.5　字数：235 千
版次：2018 年 8 月第 1 版　　2018 年 9 月第 1 次印刷

ISBN　978-7-212-10024-7　　　　　　定价：38.00 元

代 序

我们共同的日子

个人一年一度最重要的日子是生日，大家一年一度最重要的日子是节日。节日是大家共同的日子。

节日是一种纪念日，内涵多种多样。有民族的、国家的、宗教的，比如国庆节、圣诞节等。有某一类人的，如妇女、儿童、劳动者的，这便是妇女节、儿童节、劳动节等。也有与人们的生活生产密切相关的，这类节日历史悠久，很早就形成了一整套人们约定俗成、代代相传的节日习俗，这是一种传统的节日。传统节日也多种多样。中国是一个多民族国家，有 56 个民族，统称中华民族。传统节日有全民族共有的，也有某个民族特有的。比如春节、中秋节、元宵节、端午节、清明节、重阳节等，就为中华民族所共用和共享；世界文化遗产羌年就为羌族独有和独享。各民族这样的节日很多。

传统节日是在漫长的农耕时代形成的。农耕时代生产与生活、人与自然的关系十分密切。人们或为了感恩于大自然的恩赐，或为了庆祝辛勤劳作换来的收获，或为了激发生命的活力，或为了加强人际的亲情，经过长期相互认同，最终约定俗成，渐渐把一年中某一天确定为节日，并创造了十分完整又严格的节俗，如仪式、庆典、规制、禁忌，乃至特定的游艺、装饰与食品，来把节日这天演化成一个独具内涵、迷人的日子。更重要的是，人们在每一个传统的节日里，还把共同的生活理想、人间愿望与审美追求融入节日的内涵与种种仪式中。因此,它是中华民族世间理想与生活愿望极致的表现。可以说,我们的传统——精神文化传统,往往就是依靠这代代相传的一年一度的节日继承下来的。

然而,自从 20 世纪整个人类进入由农耕文明向工业文明的过渡,农耕时代形成的文化传统开始瓦解。尤其是中国,在近百年由封闭走向开放的过程中,节日文化——特别是城市的节日文化受到现代文明与外来文化的冲击。当下人们已经鲜明地感受到传统节日渐行渐远,并为此产生忧虑。传统节日的淡化必然使其中蕴含的传统精神随之涣散。然而,人们并没有坐等传统的消失,主动和积极地与之应对。这充分显示了当代中国人在文化上的自觉。

近 10 年,随着中国民间文化遗产抢救工程的全面展开,国家非物质文化遗产名录申报工作的有力推动,传统节日受到关注,一些重要的传统节日被列入了国家文化遗产名录。继而,2006 年国家将每年 6 月的第二个周六确定为"文化遗产日",2007 年国务院决定将 3 个中华民族的重要节日——清明节、端午节和中秋节列为法定放假日。这一重大决定,表现了国家对公众的传统文化生活及其传承的重视与尊重,同时也是保护节日文化遗产十分必要的措施。

节日不放假必然直接消解了节日文化,放假则是恢复节日传统的首要条件。但放假不等于远去的节日立即就会回到身边。节日与假日的不同是因为节日有特定的文化内容与文化形式。那么,重温与恢复已经变得陌生的传统节日习俗则是必不可少的了。

千百年来,我们的祖先从生活的愿望出发,为每一个节日都创造出许许多多美丽又动人的习俗。这种愿望是理想主义的，所以节日习俗是理想的；愿望是情感化的，所以节日习俗也是情感化的；愿望是美好的，所以节日习俗是美的。人们用合家团聚的年夜饭迎接新年；把天上的明月化为手中甜甜的月饼，来象征人间的团圆；在严寒刚刚消退、万物复苏的早春，赶到野外去打扫墓地，告慰亡灵，表达心中的缅怀，同时戴花插柳，踏青春游，亲切地拥抱大地山川……这些诗意化的节日习俗，使我们一代代人的心灵获得了美好的安慰与宁静。

对于少数民族来说，他们特有的节日的意义则更加重要。节日还是他们民族集体记忆的载体、共同精神的依托、个性的表现、民族身份之所在。

谁说传统的习俗过时了？如果我们淡忘了这些习俗，就一定要去重温一下传统。重温不是表象地模仿古人的形式，而是用心去体验传统中的精神与情感。

在历史进程中，习俗是在不断变化的，但民族传统的精神实质不应变。这传统就是对美好生活的不懈追求，对大自然的感恩与敬畏，对家庭团圆与世间和谐永恒的企望。

这便是我们节日的主题，也是这套《多彩中国节》丛书编写的根由与目的。

中国 56 个民族是一个大家庭，各民族的节日文化异彩纷呈，既有春节、元宵节、中秋节这样多民族共庆的节日，也有泼水节、火把节、那达慕等少数民族特有的节日。这套丛书选取了中国最有代表性的 10 个传统节日，一节一册，图文并茂，汉英对照，旨在为海内外读者通俗、全面地呈现中国绚丽多彩的节庆文化和民俗文化；放在一起则是中华民族传统节日的一部全书，既有知识性、资料性、工具性，又有可读性和趣味性。10 本精致的小册子，以翔实的文献和生动的传说，将每个节日的源起、流布与习俗，图文并茂、有滋有味地娓娓道来，从这些节日的传统中，可以看出中国人的精神追求和文化脉络。这样一套丛书不仅是对我国传统节日的一次总结，也是对传统节日文化富于创意的弘扬。

我读了书稿，心生欣喜，因序之。

冯骥才

（全国政协常委、中国文联原执行副主席）

Preface

Our Common Days

The most important day for a person is his or her birthday while the most important days for all are festivals, which are our common days.

Festivals are embedded with rich connotations for remembering. There're ethnic, national, and religious ones, such as National Day and Christmas Day; festivals for a certain group of people, such as Women's Day, Children's Day, and Laborers' Day; and those closely related to people's life and production, which enjoy a long history and feature a complete set of well-established festive traditions passed on from one generation to another. These are so-called traditional festivals, which vary greatly, too.

China, consisting of 56 nationalities, is a multi-ethnic country. People in China are collectively called the Chinese nation. So it's no wonder that some of the traditional festivals are celebrated by all nationalities while others only by certain nationalities, with the representatives of the former ones being the Spring Festival, the Lantern Festival, the Dragon Boat Festival, the Tomb-Sweeping Festival, and the Double Ninth Festival, etc. and that of the latter being the Qiang New Year, a unique festival for Qiang ethnic group. Each of ethnic groups in China has quite a number of their unique traditional festivals.

The traditional festivals have taken shape in the long agrarian times when people were greatly dependent on nature and when life was closely related to production. People gradually saw eye to eye with each other in the long-term practicing sets of rituals, celebrations, taboos as well as games, embellishments, and foods in a strict way and decided to select some days of one year as festivals with a view to expressing their gratitude to nature, celebrating harvesting, stimulating vitality of life, or strengthening bonds between family members and relatives. In this way, festivals have evolved into charming days with unique connotations. More importantly, people have instilled their common aspirations and aesthetic pursuits into festive connotations and rituals. To put it simply, festivals are consummate demonstrations of Chinese people's worldly aspirations and ideals, and Chinese people's spiritual cultures are inherited for generations by them.

Nevertheless, the cultural traditions formed in the agrarian times began to collapse with human beings being in transition from agrarian civilization to industrial one, esp., in China, whose festive cultures were severely hammered by modern civilization and foreign cultures in nearly one hundred years from being closed to opening up to the world. Nowadays, people strongly feel that traditional festivals are drifting away from their lives and are deeply concerned about it owing to the fact that dilution of traditional festivals means the fall of the traditional spirit of Chinese people. Of course, we don't wait and see; instead, we cope with it in a positive way. This fully displays the contemporary Chinese people's cultural consciousness.

In recent ten years, the traditional festivals have been earning more and more attention and some significant ones are included to the list of the National Heritages with the vigorous promotion of China's Folk Heritage Rescue Program and China's intangible cultural heritage application; for example, China set the second Saturday of June as "Cultural Heritage Day" in 2006; the State Council decided to list three significant traditional festivals as legal holidays—the Tomb-Sweeping Festival, the Dragon Boat Festival, and the Mid-Autumn Festival in 2007. These measures show the state gives priority to and pay tribute to the inheritance of public traditional cultures.

Holidays are necessary for spending festivals which will be diluted otherwise; however, holidays don't necessarily bring back traditional festivals. Since festivals, different from holidays, are equipped with special cultural forms and contents, it's essential to recover those traditional festive customs which have become stranger and stranger to contemporary Chinese people.

In the past thousands of years, our ancestors, starting from their aspirations, created many fine and engaging traditions. These aspirations are ideal, emotional, and beautiful, so are the festival traditions. People usher in the New Year by having the meal together on the New Year's Eve, make moon cakes by imitating the moon in the sky, standing for family reunion, or go to sweep the tombs of ancestors or family members for commemorating or comforting in the early spring when the winter just recedes and everything wakes up while taking spring hiking and enjoying spring scenes by the way. These poetic festive customs greatly comfort souls of people for generations.

As for ethnic minority people, their special festivals mean more to them. The festivals carry the collective memory, common spirit, character of their ethnic groups as well as mark their ethnic identities.

Are the traditional festive customs really out-dated? We're compelled to review them if we really forget them. What matters for review is not imitating the forms of the ancient Chinese people's celebrations but experiencing essence and emotions embedded in them with heart and soul.

Traditions have evolved with history's evolving, but the traditional national spirit has never changed. The spirit lies in people's never-ending pursuit for beautiful life, consistent gratitude and awe for nature, constant aspiration for family reunion and world harmony.

This is also the theme of our festivals and the root-cause of compiling the series.

The Chinese nation, featuring its colorful and varieties of festive cultures, boasts the common festivals celebrated by all nationalities, such as the Spring Festival, the Lantern Festival, the Mid-Autumn Festival, and the ethnic festivals, such as the Water Splashing Festival (Thai people), the Torch Festival (Yi people), Naadam (Mongolian nationality). This series, selecting the most typical ten festivals of China, with each festival being in one volume with figures and in both English and Chinese, unfolds the colorful festive and folk cultures in an engaging and all-round way for appealing to foreign readers. If put together, they constitute a complete set of books on Chinese traditional festivals, being instructive and intriguing. The ten brochures elaborate on the origins, distribution, and customs of each festival in an engaging way with figures, tales, and rich literature. Chinese people's spiritual pursuit and cultural veining can be tracked in this series, serving as a summary of Chinese traditional festivals and innovative promotion of them.

I went over the series with delight, and with delight, wrote the preface, too.

Feng Jicai

CPPCC National Committee member

Former Vice-president of the China Federation of Literary and Art Circles

目　录

目

录

Contents

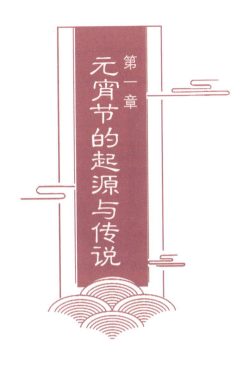

第一章

元宵节的起源与传说

按照中国传统的农历计算方法，一年的十二个月中，仅正月里就有两个对中国人来说最为重要的传统节日：春节和元宵节。从时间上看，两个节日紧紧相连。春节共持续 14 天，是从腊月三十日（除夕）到正月十四日，而正月十五日，便是元宵节。

中国地域宽广，习俗各异，所以元宵节在不同地方有不同叫法，包括"上元节"、"小正月"、"元夕"或"灯节"等称谓。正月是一年之首，在中国又称 "元月"，"宵"在古代汉语为"夜"的意思。正月十五日因为是一年中第一个月圆之夜，被人们视为大地回春的夜晚，预示着一元复始，万象更新。另外，因为元宵节在春节之后，也被中国人视为春节的最后一天，即庆祝年节的最后一天。

　　根据汉代文献记载，元宵节起源于 2000 多年前的西汉（公元前 202 年—公元 9 年），内容都与汉代某个皇帝相关。另外，关于元宵节的起源也有与宗教或某个习俗相关的说法。

　　关于元宵节，有着许多的传说。

一、
汉文帝纪念平定"诸吕之乱"

　　根据中国的历史记载和民俗传说，汉朝（西汉）开国皇帝高祖刘邦（公元前 256 年—前 195 年）去世后，吕皇后的儿子刘盈登基，称汉惠帝。但他生性懦弱，不擅于朝政，国家权力渐渐由吕后来掌控（公元前 195 年—前 180 年）。吕皇后病逝后，其亲信惶惶不安，害怕遭到迫害。为了自保，上将军吕产、吕禄召集同谋策划夺取刘氏江山。造反还未实施，便被刘氏宗室齐王刘襄得知。为保住刘氏江山，他带着一些大臣起兵讨伐吕禄，平定了"诸吕之乱"。之后，众大臣拥立刘邦的第二个儿子刘恒登基，称汉文帝（公元前 180 年—前 157 年）。文帝深感太平盛世来之不易，便把平息"诸吕之乱"的正月十五定为与民同乐的重要日子。自此以后，文帝会在每年的正月十五这一天夜晚出宫游玩，与民同乐，后来他下令将正月十五命名为元宵节。

二、
汉武帝祭祀"太一"神

与上述传说不同，有人称元宵节与汉武帝相关。

"太一"，是主宰世界万事万物的天神，拥有至高无上的权威。秦朝时，即称为太皇，与天皇、地皇并称三皇，是秦汉时流行的三个天神，但是把太一神提高到至尊的地位，成为汉统治者尊奉的天帝神，是汉武帝的功劳。汉武帝时（公元前156年—前87年），西汉社会已得到恢复发展，由于削弱了诸侯王的势力，中央集权日益加强，在政治上已出现大一统的局面。武帝即位时，还有五帝崇拜的传统，缺乏至上神的观念，不利于中央政权的巩固。元光二年（公元前133年），有一个名叫谬忌的方士，奏请祭祀

○汉武帝

太一神，明确提出五帝只是太一神之佐，突出了太一是至上神的地位。汉武帝采纳了这个建议，下令在长安东南郊立了太一坛，按谬忌的方案祭祀。元鼎四年（公元前 113 年）在汾阳（今山西河津南）出土一个古鼎，公卿大臣视为宝鼎，都认为是一种祥瑞。汉武帝下令将它迎至甘泉。元鼎五年（公元前 112 年），汉武帝正式在甘泉建立太一祭坛，坛分三层，由于五帝是太一的辅佐，所以他们的坛环绕在下面，青、赤、白、黑四帝，各按东西南北方排定，只有黄帝坛，置于西南方。同年十一月，汉武帝举行隆重的郊祀，亲自祭拜太一神，正式钦命太一为汉家至尊的上帝神。第二年，汉武帝以祭天礼仪亲自到太一坛祭祀。至此，太一作为汉王朝至高至尊的国神，终于被塑造成功。有了这一传统，每年的正月十五，汉武帝都要在自己的皇宫中祭祀"太一"，后人便有了在正月十五祭祀天神的习俗。

　　除了有帝王与节日起源相关外，也有元宵节与佛教、道教等宗教相关的传说。

三、
汉明帝点灯敬佛

　　东汉（公元 25 年—220 年）是中国历史上大力倡导并推行佛教的时期，这与汉明帝（公元 28 年—75 年）有直接的关系。传说明帝在位期间,有一天,他梦见一个金人,有4米8(一丈六尺)高,脖子上佩戴着一个太阳般闪亮的光圈。这个光圈光芒四射,金光灿烂,金人在金銮殿上各处飞行。明帝梦醒以后感到非常奇怪,就把梦中所见事情告诉太史傅毅。傅说:"传说西方有个神,名字叫佛,陛下您所梦见的就是佛。"那时候所谓的西方指的就是印度。于是明帝就派遣蔡愔、秦景、王遵等十八人到印度去请佛。路上经过大月氏国即今天阿富汗国境内,正巧遇到了摄摩腾、竺法兰二位法师,骑着两匹白马,带着佛像和佛的舍利以及梵文贝叶经六十万言。两位尊者不辞劳顿,历经万难,跟随这十八位使者终于在永平十年(公元67年)抵达洛阳。明帝非常钦敬尊者以弘法为志的精神,特别以国礼接待,把二位尊者迎接到洛阳,先住鸿胪寺,不久又在洛阳雍门外修建了一座规模宏大的白马寺,作为二位尊者翻译经典的场所。从白马寺始,中国的僧院便泛称为寺,白马寺也因此被认为是中国佛教的发源地。

○白马寺

白 马 寺

白马寺，位于河南省洛阳老城以东 12 公里处，始建于东汉永平十一年（公元 68 年），是佛教传入中国后兴建的第一座寺院。白马寺建立之后，中国"僧院"便泛称为"寺"，白马寺也因此被认为是中国佛教的发源地，有中国佛教的"祖庭"和"释源"之称。寺内保存了大量元代夹纻干漆造像如三世佛、二天将、十八罗汉等，弥足珍贵。1961 年，白马寺被中华人民共和国国务院公布为第一批全国重点文物保护单位之一。

开放时间：全年开放，每日 07:30—19:00

门票价格：50 元

著名景点：万国佛殿区、齐云塔、清凉台

适宜游玩季节：4—5 月、9—11 月

交通：坐飞机抵达河南郑州新郑机场，乘高铁、大巴或火车到洛阳，改乘公交车即达。

白马东来后，蔡愔等人称印度摩喝陀国每逢正月十五，僧众云集瞻仰佛舍利，点灯敬佛，是参佛的吉日良辰，汉明帝对此非常崇敬，下令正月十五夜在宫中和寺院挂灯敬佛，士族庶民都要挂灯以表示对佛的尊敬。汉代长安城有保卫京城和宫城的官员专门负责宵禁，但在正月十五夜晚，皇帝特许他们休息，前后各一日，允许士族庶民踏月观灯。此后，元宵节放灯的习俗就由宫廷流传到民间，元宵逐渐成为民间盛大的节日。一般人家都要在佛堂点灯，上香，用水果等来供佛，同时，还要组织举行龙灯、狮子灯、茶灯、鱼灯、马灯等"灯戏""灯舞"游戏庆祝。这些庆典活动演变成以供灯敬佛为主要内容的节日，其形式也基本上得以固定下来。这种以佛教礼仪为主要内容的正月十五便成为元宵节，兴起了赏灯习俗。这便是"元宵节张灯""元宵节观灯"的起源。

四、东方朔暗助元宵姑娘

也有一种说法，说是元宵节的来由与汉武帝时的一位宠臣东方朔有关。

东方朔是个非常有才干、善良风趣的人。有一年的冬天，大雪飘落了好多天，皇宫御花园中的梅花开得非常鲜艳。东方朔想折一些梅花送给汉武帝，刚进御花园的门，就看见一个泪流满面的宫女，正准备投井自尽，东方朔急忙上前搭救。随后，姑娘告诉了他自尽的原因。

姑娘的名字叫元宵，从小就离开了父母和妹妹进宫做宫女，后来就再也没有与家人团聚过。每年春节来临之时，她就更加思念家人。

这一年她又没有机会回家孝敬父母，心里非常难过，对生活也绝望了，便起了轻生的念头。听了元宵姑娘的遭遇，东方朔非常同情她，也为她的孝心感动了。他决定帮助她，并向她保证一定会想办法让她与家人团聚。

有一天，东方朔出了皇宫，在长安街上摆了一个占卜的摊位，街上的很多行人都来向他求卦。奇怪的是，每个人占的签语都是"正月十六火焚身"。接下来的一段时间里，东方朔都在街上替人占卜，而所占到的都是"正月十六火焚身"的内容，引起了长安城里很多人的恐慌。当人们向东方朔寻求解灾方法时，他说："正月十五日的傍晚，火神君会派一位赤衣神女下凡查访。她奉旨要烧了长安城，如果不能制止，正月十六长安城就会有一场大灾难。现在唯一可以想办法来制止的人就只有当今天子了。"东方朔还把这些偈语抄在红纸条上，散发在长安城的街道上，老百姓们拿着红帖，送到皇宫禀报皇上。

红帖传到汉武帝手里。大臣们知晓此事后，纷纷发表意见。当汉武帝询问东方朔时，他假意思考了一下说，"听说火神君最爱吃汤圆，宫里的宫女元宵不是经常给万岁做汤圆吗？十五晚上可让她做好汤圆，万岁焚香上供，然后也传令京城里的百姓们家家都做汤圆，一齐敬奉给火神君，让他忘记自己最初的命令。另外，还需要让臣民们在正月十五的晚上挂上灯笼，在长安城里点鞭炮、放烟火，这样就可以让天上的神仙们误认为长安城已被焚毁，也就可以瞒过掌管人间一切的玉帝了。然后，通知城外的老百姓，让他们来城里观灯，这样就可以消灾解难了。"

汉武帝听了东方朔的意见，觉得非常有道理，大臣们也一致认为这一方法可行，最后皇帝便传旨照东方朔的办法去做。一转眼就到了正月十五日，长安城里张灯结彩，汉武帝带了妃子、宫娥离开皇宫，与臣民们一起游长安街。他们一边游玩，一边放鞭炮、放礼花。

整个长安街灯火通明，热闹非常。宫女元宵的父母也带着妹妹进城观灯，当他们看到一些宫灯上写着"元宵"两个字时，止不住惊喜地喊着"元宵！元宵！"这时，与其他宫女一起在街上游玩的元宵听到了父母的呼喊，跟随着声音的方向找到了家人，终于与家人相聚了。

○ 元宵姑娘

　　如此热闹了一夜，长安城果然平安无事，也没有被火神君焚烧。汉武帝非常高兴，就下令以后汉朝的臣民们每年正月十五日都要做汤圆供奉给火神君，在城里面要挂灯放烟火。元宵姑娘从此以后每年都能在正月十五这一天出宫与家人团聚，而汉武帝觉得她做的汤圆很好吃，便把正月十五这天命名为元宵节。

五、
"破镜重圆"的故事

南北朝时期陈朝末代皇帝陈叔宝（公元 583 年—589 年）有个才貌双全的妹妹乐昌公主，嫁给太子舍人徐德言为妻。眼看陈朝要灭亡，徐德言担心亡国后夫妻两人会离散，便与乐昌公主商定，打破一面铜镜，各拿一半，作为以后相见的凭证，并约定元宵节在街市上卖镜。不久之后，陈朝果然被隋朝所灭。隋文帝将乐昌公主赐给了功臣杨素做小妾。虽然杨素非常宠爱乐昌公主，但是乐昌公主心里一直惦记着自己的相公徐德言，终日郁郁寡欢。

第二年的正月十五，经历了浩劫的徐德言匆匆来到街市，到处寻找卖镜的人。功夫不负有心人，在一个街角果然看见了一个老头在叫卖半片铜镜，而且价钱相当

○绘本《乐昌公主》作者：萧竹

昂贵，令街市上的人不敢问津。徐德言一看到是半片铜镜，连忙按老人所要的价钱买下了这半面镜子，又邀请老人到自己的住处。徐德言向老人讲述了自己与乐昌公主破镜的故事，并拿出自己的另外一面铜镜。老人被他们的故事感动了，承诺一定要为他们传递消息。

老人没有食言，想尽办法把消息传到了乐昌公主那里。乐昌公主得到了丈夫的消息，更加伤悲，终日不吃不喝。杨素关心她，耐心询问缘由，知道其中的故事后，便想要成人之美。他派人把徐德言召入府中，让他与公主团聚，并带着她回归故里。因此，便就有了破镜重圆的典故，流传至今。元宵节也就有了"亲人团圆"之意。

也有人说元宵节与道教的"三元"有关。元宵节又称为上元节。这里的"上元"出自中国道教的说法，含有新的一年第一次月圆之夜的意思。五斗米教（天师道）是道教早期的重要流派，起源于东汉时期。五斗米教崇奉的神为天官、地官、水官，并以三元配三官，说上元天官正月十五日生，中元地官七月十五日生，下元水官十月十五日生。因此，道教就把一年中的正月十五称为上元节，七月十五为中元节，十月十五为下元节，合称"三元"。

Chapter One

The Legends about the Origin of the Lantern Festival

According to the Chinese lunar calendar, of the twelve months in a year, the first lunar month has the two most important traditional festivals for all Chinese people: the Spring Festival and the Lantern Festival, and they are very close in time. The Spring Festival or Chinese New Year always comes in the 1st day of the first lunar month, but its celebrations usually start from the New Year's Eve or Chuxi to the 14th day of the first lunar month. And the Lantern Festival just falls on the 15th day of the month.

China has a large territory, and customs are various in different places. That's why the Lantern Festival has different names in different places, such as Shang Yuan Festival (the First Full-Moon Day), Small Festival in the 1st Lunar Month, Yuan Xi(the Night of the first Full-moon Month), and Yuan Xiao Festival (the day to eat yuanxiao, a kind of sweet dumpling made of glutinous rice flour). In China, the first lunar month is called Yuan Month, representing the beginning of a year; Xiao means night in ancient Chinese language. The 15th night of Yuan month is the first full-month night of a year, symbolizing the coming

back of spring and the refreshing of all lives. Since it closely followed the Spring Festival, the Lantern Festival is also regarded as the last day of Spring Festival celebrations.

As recorded in the Han Dynasty document, the Lantern Festival originated from an emperor of the Western Han Dynasty (202 BC ~ 9 AD). Other documents also said that its origin is related to religion or an ancient custom.

More legends about the Lantern Festival are as follows.

1. Commemoration of the End of Lv Clan Disturbance by Emperor Wen of Han

As Chinese historical records and folklores say, after the death of Liu Bang, the first emperor of the Han Dynasty (256 BC-195 BC), the Empress Lv (reigning from 195 BC to 180 BC) took charge of state power because their son Liu Ying, Emperor Hui, was too indecisive to deal with the state affairs. When Empress Lv died of disease, her political clans were all desperate to seek self-protection, thus upper-general Lv Chan and Lv Lu called their people to plot a rebellion. That plot was discovered by Prince Liu Nang, a royal member of Liu Clan, who was united with some other officials and mounted an expedition against the Lv Clan Disturbance. Soon, Liu Heng, the second son of Liu Bang ascended the throne and proclaimed himself as Emperor Wen (reigning from 180 BC to 157 BC). Considering the hard-earned peace and prosperity, Emperor Wen decided to commemorate the ending of the Lv Clan Disturbance on the 15th day of the first lunar month. Yearly on that night, Emperor Wen would leave the palace to enjoy the full moon with common people, and later he designated the day as Lantern Festival.

2. Worship of Taiyi God by Emperor Wu of Han

Some other people believe that the Lantern Festival is related to Emperor Wu of Han Dynasty.

Taiyi is the God of Heaven in ancient Chinese legend, who has the superb power to control the world. Taiyi, also called Superb God, together with Heavenly God and Earthly God, are respected as the Three Gods in the Qin-Han Dynasties. It was Emperor Wu who proclaimed Taiyi God as the most respected and worshiped god in heaven. In the reign of Emperor Wu (156 BC—87 BC), the society had gained recovery in economy, the power of feudal princes were reduced, and a centralized government was taking its shape. At the beginning of Wu's reign, the tradition of worshiping the Five Holy Emperors was the biggest obstacle for unification of the state, thus Wu tried his best to promote worshiping the Superb God Taiyi above the Five Holy Emperors. In 133 BC, a Taoist priest named Miuji wrote a memorial to the throne saying that the Five Holy Emperors were actually the assistants of Taiyi God, and Taiyi should be respected as the Superb God. Emperor Wu approved that suggestion and built a Taiyi Temple in the southeast suburb of Chang'an City (the present Xi'an). In 113 BC, an old tripod was unearthed in Fenyang (today's south Hejin of Shanxi Province), which was believed an auspicious sign and was officially sent to Ganquan. In 112 BC, Emperor Wu officially opened the three-layer Taiyi Temple, surrounded by the temples for the Five Holy Emperors with Green Emperor, Red Emperor, White Emperor and Black Emperor at the east, west, south and north respectively, only Yellow Emperor at the southwest. In November, Emperor Wu held a grand sacrifice to Taiyi God and officially claimed Taiyi as the Superb God. In the next year, Emperor Wu went to Taiyi Temple in person to pray to the Heaven with the grandest sacrifice. Since then, Taiyi had finally become the Superb God of the Han Dynasty. On each 15th night of the first lunar month, Emperor Wu would hold sacrifices to Taiyi in the royal palace, which is regarded as the origin of sacrifice ceremony on the Lantern Festival. Later Han people come out to enjoy colorful lanterns at the full-moon night of the first lunar month."

Apart from the links between emperors and its origin, the Lantern Festival has something to do with religions, like Buddhism and Taoism.

3. Emperor Ming Lighting a Lantern to Worship Budda

Buddhism gained rapid development during the Eastern Han Dynasty (25 AD—220 AD) thanks to Emperor Ming. It is said that one night Emperor Ming dreamt that a golden man about was flying around the royal palace who wore a shining golden ring around his neck. On the next morning, Emperor Ming felt puzzled about his dream and asked his court historian Fu Yi, "What omen is that?" Fu replied, "People say there is a god in the west, named Budda. I think what Your Majesty dreamed is Budda." The west at that time refers to India. Emperor Ming sent out 18 emissaries to India to invite Budda. When the emissaries arrived in the Great Yuezhi (today's Afghanistan), they happened to meet She Moteng and Zhu Falan, two Buddhist masters on two white horses, who were carrying along Budda statues, Buddhist relics and Sanskrit

Palm-Leaf Manuscripts of over 600,000 words. Hearing of their intentions, the two masters decided to follow the 18 emissaries to go to Luoyang. And finally after a hard journey they arrived in Luoyang City in 67 AD Emperor Ming was greatly impressed by the strong will of the two masters, and received them with the state-guest etiquettes in Honglu Temple. Later, Ming ordered to build a grand White Horse Temple for the two masters as a holy place for manuscripts translation. Since then, all the Buddhist monasteries have been called *si* (meaning temple) in Chinese, and White Horse Temple is regarded as the cradle of Chinese Buddhism.

Tips for Tourism

White Horse Temple

White Horse Temple, located 12 km in the east of Laocheng District, Luoyang of Henan Province, was built in 68 AD as the first Buddhist temple after Buddhism was introduced into China. Since then, China's monasteries had been called temples, and White Horse Temple was regarded as the cradle of Buddhism in China. It has kept numerous valuable figures of Buddha. In 1961, White Horse Temple was listed into the first patch of national cultural relics protection departments.

Opening hours: 7:30−19:00, all year round

Ticket price:50 RMB

Famous scenic spots:

Peak seasons: April, May, September, October and November

Routes: Tourists can fly to Xinzhen Airport, take high-speed rails, coaches or trains to Luoyang, and then transfer buses to get to the temple.

Later, the 18 emissaries reported that in India the 15th

night of the first lunar month was an auspicious time to pray to Buddha, and all the monks would light up lanterns to worship the Buddhist relics. Emperor Ming respected the tradition and ordered to light up lanterns in temples, palaces, mansions and houses to show worship to Buddha. In Chang'an City, the capital of both Western and Eastern Han Dynasties, curfew was carried at night except for the 15th night of first lunar month. Even on the 14th and 16th night, people were allowed to go out and watch the lanterns under the full moon. Gradually the lantern tradition became a grand celebration for common people. In common people's houses, they would light up lanterns, burn incense, and sacrifice fruits to worship Buddha. Some lantern dramas and lantern dances would be put on for celebration, with different images of lanterns, such as dragon lantern, lion lantern, tea lantern, fish lantern, and horse lantern. Those celebrations are carried on and developed into the Lantern Festival. Chinese people will raise up lanterns and watch lantern shows to celebrate the festival.

4. Dongfang Shuo and Maid Yuan Xiao

Some people say that the Lantern Festival has something to do with Dongfang Shuo, a favored official of Emperor Wu in the Han Dynasty.

Dongfang was a capable, honest and humorous man. On a winter day after a heavy snow, he wanted to pick some snowy plum blossom for the Emperor, but as soon as he stepped into the imperial garden, he saw a maid crying broken-heartedly who was about to jump into a well. He immediately stopped the girl from committing suicide. The girl then told him her story.

She was named Yuan Xiao. She never had the chance to meet her family after she became a maid in the imperial palace. When the Spring Festival came around, she could not help missing her parents and younger sister. She thought she wouldn't have had a chance to go back home, thus she became desperate about her future life. Having heard Yuan's story, Dongfang was moved by her love for parents and decided to help her reunite with her family.

One day, Dongfang went out of palace and set a stall to practice divination. Many passers-by asked divination from him and strangely enough, all the fortune telling sticks said the same sentence "Trapped in a big fire on the 16th day of the first lunar month." The same situation continued for several days, and all the people in the city became panic-stricken and swarmed to him for solution. He replied, "On the evening of the 15th day of the first lunar month, the God of Fire will send a goddess in red to come to the mortal world and burn the Chang'an City. If no one could stop her, the whole city would be in a disaster. The only one who can save us is our emperor." Dongfang wrote the sentence on some red fly sheets and scattered them in the streets. The people collected those red fly sheets and sent them to the imperial palace.

When Emperor Wu read the red sheet, he asked all the ministers to give opinions. Dongfang pretended to ponder for a while and said, "I heard the God of Fire likes to eat sweet dumplings. Luckily the maid Yuan Xiao is good at making them. We can ask Yuan Xiao to prepare and sacrifice them to the God of Fire. All the common people should do the same. When the God of Fire is satisfied with the meal, he would forget his initial intention. Besides, we need to light up lanterns, set off firecrackers and fireworks on the evening, which will give the gods a false impression that the city has been burnt down, and open the gates of the city to have the people outside come in for lantern display. Only in this way can the disaster be avoided."

Emperor Wu and all the official ministers all agreed upon it. On the 15th night of the first lunar month, Chang'an City was lit up with colorful lanterns. Emperor Wu together with his wives and maids left the palace to join the parade to watch the lantern display, setting off fireworks and crackers on the way. The whole city was in a splendid brightness and excitement. Yuan Xiao's parents and sister were among the crowds when they saw the characters "Yuan Xiao" on some palace lanterns, they couldn't help shouting out, "Yuan Xiao! Yuan Xiao!" The maid Yuan Xiao recognized her parents'voice and turned to look for them. Finally the family got reunion.

When the night was over, the city was absolutely safe and sound, no fire at all. Emperor Wu was very delighted and ordered all the people to prepare sweet dumplings for the God of Fire, and to light up lanterns and set off fireworks on that day of every year. And Yuan Xiao could go out of palace and see her family once a year. Thanks to her good skill in making sweet dumplings, Emperor Wu crowned the 15th day of the first lunar month as Yuan Xiao Festival.

5. The Story of A Broken Mirror

In the late Chen Dynasty, the Emperor Chen Shubao (reigning from 583AD to 589AD) married his sister Princess Lechang to Xu Deyan, an assistant minister of Crown Prince. Seeing the Chen Dynasty would perish soon, Xu and Lechang worried about a possible separation in the wartime, thus they broke a mirror, each one holding a half as a signal for future reunion at the next Lantern Festival fair. Later the Chen Dynasty was replaced by the Sui Dynasty, and Emperor Wen of Sui granted Princess Lechang to be a concubine of Yang Su, a meritorious minister. Though she was favored by Yang, Lechang still could not forget her first husband Xu, and seldom felt happy.

On the next Lantern Festival night, Xu Deyan went through a great hard time and hurried to the fair. After a careful search, he finally found the half broken mirror which was being sold at an unreasonable high price by an old man. Xu paid for the broken mirror and invited the old man to his dwelling place. Xu showed him the other half mirror and shared his love story. The old man was moved and promised to deliver messages between them.

The old man kept his words and managed to contact Princess Lechang. Hearing of his husband's message, she could not help crying all day long, with no heart for dinner. Yang Su asked her the reason and decided to let the couple meet again. He sent soldiers to take Xu into his residence to meet Lechang, and finally agreed to let the loved couple go back to their homeland. The romantic story of the broken mirror has been handed down to the present, and the Lantern Festival has become a time for family reunion since then.

It is said that Lantern Festival has its origins in Taoism. Lantern Festival is also called Shang Yuan Festival. "Shang Yuan" comes from China's indigenous Taoism, meaning the first full-moon night in a year. There was a Taoist movement called Way of the Five Pecks of Rice or the Celestial Masters in the Eastern Han Dynasty. The Celestial Masters believed three Taoist gods, Tianguan giving blessing, Diguan absolving the guilty, and Shuiguan relieving misfortune; Tianguan's birthday falls on the 15th day of the first lunar month, Diguan on the 15th day of the seventh lunar month, Shuiguan on the 15th day of the tenth lunar month. Taoism thus gave the three days a respective name, Shang Yuan Festival, Zhong Yuan Festival and Xia Yuan Festival.

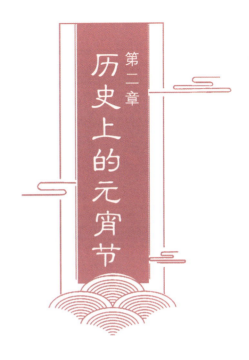

第二章
历史上的元宵节

在中国历史上，各个时代的元宵节习俗有所不同，在节日的时间上，围绕着正月十五这一天，也有长有短。

汉朝（公元前202年—公元220年）时节期为一天。唐朝（公元618年—907年）为三天。宋朝（公元960年—1279年）延长到五天。明朝（公元1368年—1644年）则从正月初八开始点灯，到正月十七日的夜里才把灯熄灭。明朝元宵节的节期与春节相接，人们白天逛市，晚上观灯，非常热闹。到了清朝（公元1644年—1912年），各地元宵节的民俗活动更加丰富，节期却缩短到了三至五天。民国时期（公元1912年—1949年），规定元宵节为三天，这一节期至今在中国一些地方还保留着，而一些地方元宵节仅为正月十五这一天。

元宵节的习俗随着历史的发展越来越丰富多彩。正月十五点灯的习俗源于汉朝。到了唐代，赏灯的习俗更加兴盛，皇宫中、街道上、百姓家处处挂灯，在皇城中还建有高大的灯轮、灯楼和灯树等。唐宋时期的元宵节灯市还兴起了杂耍。明清两代，元宵节中已经发展了猜灯谜活动，还有百戏歌舞、戏曲表演等更加丰富的习俗。到了现代，元宵节已成为中国人的重要传统节日，各地的节庆活动各不相同，不少地方结合了本地的风俗习惯，增加了耍龙灯、耍狮子、踩高跷、划旱船、扭秧歌、打太平鼓等传统民俗表演。

一、
隋朝元宵节

隋朝非常注重元宵节，所以元宵节在这一时期完全形成。隋文帝（公元541年—604年）统一天下后，安定了混乱的政治局面，社会逐渐得到发展和繁荣，元宵节也被定为一年一度狂欢庆祝的重要日子。《隋书·柳彧传》中大臣柳彧记载所见的元宵庆典："城内外灯火明亮，鼓声回荡在街头，人们化装游行，还有杂技表演等活动。"

隋文帝的儿子隋炀帝（公元569年—618年）喜好奢华的生活，

执政时期恢复了元宵节的活动，还借元宵节来炫耀国强民富。每年的正月十五这天，他就在皇宫举行盛大的晚会，招待万国的来宾和使节，也命人在都城中挂灯，准备各种表演活动，让老百姓来观赏。《隋书·音乐志》中这样记载："元宵庆典甚为隆重，处处张灯结彩，日夜歌舞奏乐，表演者有3万余众，奏乐者有18,000多人，戏台有8里之长，游玩观灯的百姓更是不计其数，通宵达旦，尽情欢乐，热闹非常。"《隋书·炀帝纪》也记载：隋炀帝大业六年（公元610年）的正月十五夜，好大喜功的隋炀帝为了显示皇朝的声威，炫耀国力强盛、富足，邀请了西域的少数民族使者和商人来到洛阳。从正月十五夜晚开始，在皇城端门外的大街上搭建了大型的戏台，表演百戏。戏台周围五千步之内，18,000人奏乐，演奏的声音在数里之外都能听见。满城挂着的灯笼照亮了皇城的上空，如同白昼，这一次的元宵节一直延续了十五天。隋炀帝还下令营造一个非常繁荣的洛阳城，于是把城内外树木和花草都用绸帛缠饰，卖菜的商家要用龙须席铺地。另外，他还命令皇城中的百姓必须穿上华丽服装，没有好衣服的穷人则不准上街，不然要被抓去坐牢。西域的使节和商人如果走到饭馆门前，主人要主动邀请他们入座，喝醉吃饱了才让出门，且不准收取分文，然后吹嘘说："中国富足，饭店酒食照例不要钱。"使节和商人们深知隋朝的民情，便也故意说："中国也有衣不蔽体的穷人，为何不将缠树绸帛做成衣服给他们穿呢？"

二、唐朝元宵节

　　元宵节中挂灯的习俗，在唐朝发展成为盛况空前的灯市。唐朝中期之后，元宵节成为全民性的狂欢节。当时，首都长安严格实行宵禁，但在元宵节的三天中，取消宵禁的限制，以方便人们放灯赏灯，因此也称为"放夜"。在这三天中，王公贵族和黎民百姓们都会外出赏灯，以至于长安街车水马龙，人潮汹涌，异常热闹。唐玄宗时期（公元712年—756年），皇帝让人做了巨型的灯楼，截面30尺见方，高150尺，楼身用丝绸缠裹，楼顶上高悬着龙腾虎跃的动物形象，檐角上"悬珠玉金银，微风一至，锵然成韵"，远远看上去，灯光璀璨，非常壮观。

　　唐朝时期很好地发展了灯市，朝廷不惜巨资搭建了灯轮、灯树和灯楼等，还设计了新型的巧夺天工、精美绝伦的花灯，民间的庆祝活动也越来越盛大。

　　除了灯市的发展，唐朝元宵节中的歌舞百戏更加让人目不暇接。表演歌舞的都是宫中外貌出众、能歌善舞的宫女们。皇宫要花很多钱为她们准备服装，如头上要戴着花冠，身上要穿霞帔。

　　唐代民间的元宵节兴起了一种"牵钩"，即现在所说的拔河。在

○唐朝都城的盛景

中国的古代，拔河的起源不是作为一种竞技游戏，而是求甘雨、祈年丰、期吉祥。朝廷举办声势浩大的拔河比赛，是为了表现国力的强盛，向百姓及外国使者显示王朝的强大。

二、
宋朝元宵节

　　宋朝的元宵节在节期上比唐朝多了两天。自宋太祖乾德五年（公元 967 年）开始，节期增加为五天，即多了正月十七、十八两夜，另外，节日的规模也扩大了。官民同乐是宋朝皇帝们过元宵节的宗旨，元宵节之夜,皇帝与大臣们共同参加酒宴。宋徽宗时期(公元 1100 年—1126 年),皇帝会在元宵节的夜晚带着妃嫔到宣德楼上赏灯。每个在楼下仰窥"圣颜"的仕女,皇帝都会向其赐酒一杯。据说有个女子喝了赐酒后偷藏金杯,士兵发现后将她押送到御前盘问,那女子情急之中,即诵一首词:"月满蓬壶灿烂灯,与郎携手至端门。贪看鹤阵笙歌举,不觉鸳鸯失却群。天渐晓,感皇恩,传宣赐酒饮杯巡。归家恐被翁姑责,窃取金杯作照凭。"皇帝一听,龙颜大悦,便把金杯赏赐给了她。

　　节期延长了,宋朝的商人们不失时机推出了各种新型的彩灯,来符合灯市的需求。与唐朝相比,灯的制作工艺与样式都更胜一筹。据宋朝文人孟元老在其《东京梦华录》记载,宋朝皇宫中搭建的灯山非常壮观,上面有文殊菩萨骑狮、普贤菩萨骑白象等装饰,且是用彩色丝织品结成。制作灯的工匠们独出心裁,用辘轳绞水的原理设计出特殊的动态效果,如菩萨的手臂可以摇动,手指纤细逼真,

○赏灯、猜灯谜

过水则会留痕。因为宋朝的皇帝喜欢赏灯，各地的县官为投其所好，在元宵节来临的时候，就纷纷献上各具特色的灯饰，如苏州的五色玻璃灯、福州的白玉灯、新安的无骨灯等都非常新奇。各色彩灯中，最大的是五色玻璃灯，直径达三四尺，灯上绘有山水、人物、花卉、翎毛等，栩栩如生。

正月十五的晚上是元宵活动最为丰富的时候。灯市中人山人海，人们争看花灯、歌舞和杂艺。皇城中所有酒楼茶馆都争相挂灯，鼓乐喧天。花灯的式样也尤为丰富，有"钟馗捉鬼""福禄寿星"等人物灯，桃、李、葡萄等样式的果品灯；鹿、鹤等飞禽走兽灯。节日中，穿着节日盛装的男女老少，或设宴纵饮，或拥炉谈笑，直到天明。

元宵节中，民间有一个重要的表演内容，称为"舞队"。舞队的表演活动从正月初一的春节持续到正月十六的元宵节。舞队中的人戴着面具乔装成各种人物进行表演，他们的表演主要通过滑稽的装扮和肢体动作来使观看的人们发笑。这一节日活动经过不同时代的发展延续了下来，在今天中国各地的元宵节中，也有表演队伍装扮成各种故事传说或戏剧中的角色在公共场合进行表演。

北宋初，元宵节中加入了猜灯谜活动，使得节日习俗更加丰富。灯谜就是将谜语贴在花灯上，让人一面赏灯，一面猜谜。由于谜底不易猜中，就像老虎不易被射中一样，所以灯谜也称"灯虎"。元宵节猜灯谜的民俗活动一直延续至今。

宋朝的元宵节活动如此丰富，使得那些平日里足不出户的妇女们在节日中显得非常兴奋，因此，出门之前也要精心打扮。元宵节中妇女的打扮较为独特，因为要在月亮之下出行，为了衬托皎洁的月光，她们所穿的服饰均为白色，头饰各具特色。有文献记载，通常这一夜总是有盛装的女子在拥挤的人潮中丢失自己的饰品，夜深时总能看见有人提着灯笼照路来拾遗，耳环、头饰、项链等随便都能捡到。

四、
明朝元宵节

　　明朝时期，元宵节的节期最长，从正月初八持续到十七日，共
10 天，习俗也是以灯会为主。明成祖永乐七年（公元 1409 年），皇
帝下诏给文武百官从正月十一开始放假十日。

　　与其他朝代不同的是，明朝元宵节盛行"走桥摸钉祛除百病"
的习俗。"走桥"的字面意思为过桥，即在正月十六日的夜里，京城
的妇女们要结伴在街市上游
玩，到了有桥的地方，大家相
互扶着通过，这样就能消除百
病，所以又叫"走百病"。那
些不能过桥的人，就不能长寿。
另外，"摸钉"的意思是在"走
百病"的过程中一定要经过正
阳门（北京前门），然后要摸
门上的铜钉，这样才可以生个
男孩。这一习俗在清朝也较为
盛行。

○《明宪宗元宵行乐图》

关于明朝的元宵节，一幅流传至今的《上元灯彩图》生动地再现了明代都城金陵元宵佳节的热闹场面。画卷中呈现了两千多个各具神态的人物，描绘了明万历年间（公元1573年—1620年）秦淮河往北过三山街内桥一带的元宵节盛况。从画卷中可以看出，当时的花灯种类众多，街市拥挤，非常热闹。沿街的店铺中家家都挂着五颜六色的彩灯。大街上还有卖艺的人，周围站着众多的围观者，他们神情专注，脸上带着愉悦的表情，还有人在鼓掌。穿着富贵的达官贵人们身后跟着众多仆人，老百姓也结伴游街。画卷上有一个形象逼真的龙灯，龙身由若干个灯笼相连而成，流光溢彩，渲染出元宵灯节的喜庆氛围。画中几个小男孩点着烟花爆竹，栩栩如生。

○《上元灯彩图》

五、
清朝元宵节

满族入主中原建立清朝之后，民间元宵节的节期缩短到了五天。宫廷中的元宵节节期则与民间有所不同。据皇家档案《世祖章皇帝实录》记载："上元节自正月十四日始至十六日止"。皇帝在元宵节中的主要活动是在后宫妃嫔和满朝大臣的陪同下设宴席款待外藩。之后，便在紫禁城乾清宫或圆明园正大光明、山高水长等处观灯、放焰火。

○历史悠久的自贡灯会

○哈尔滨冰灯节

　　冰灯只能在冬季制作，主要流行于中国的东北地区，元宵节中有赏冰灯的习俗，也被称为"冰灯节"。

　　另外，紫禁城内在元宵节时还有一种特殊的灯叫鳌山灯，这种灯在宋代就有。鳌山是上古神话传说中的海中高山。根据传说，再加上一些新的创意，人们设计了大型鳌山灯。它的造型为一只巨大的鳌，其背上有高山，山上有石、有树，挂着数百盏花灯，点缀着各种神像。山上有乐队在上面奏乐，也可进行歌舞表演。整个鳌山灯俨然一个神境中才会出现的华丽舞台，气势磅礴，灯光璀璨，奢华无比。皇宫的大臣们把能与皇帝一起观看鳌山灯作为一种殊荣。

　　除了宫廷灯，民间的灯也加入了更多的创意。民间的元宵节灯会中有一种会发出声音的灯，做灯的人在头一年的秋天就要养着一些蟋蟀，等到来年元宵节的时候把蟋蟀放到灯里面去。赏灯者便可一边赏灯，一边听虫鸣的声音，颇有一番情趣。

　　与灯相关，清朝宫廷中元宵节的又一特色便是大型的灯舞。据记载，表演舞灯的人最多时候有三千，她们高唱着《太平歌》，每人提一盏彩灯，按照指令信号，三千人排成一个"太"字，再转成"平"字，依次作"万"字"岁"字，又依次合成"太平万岁"字样。灯舞结束

○南京夫子庙元宵灯会

之后，便要燃放烟火。烟火声、奏乐声、嬉笑声交织着，火光映红了天际。而民间元宵节较有特色的是舞龙灯，是中国北方与南方都有的习俗。舞的龙灯通常为两条，根据龙的长度大小来配备舞龙的人数，其中必有一人操纵龙珠，演出双龙抢珠的剧情。只见两条龙随着舞龙者的动作在空中翻转飞腾，观众们的情绪也随之翻腾不已。

　　与观灯相映成趣的是燃放烟火，宫廷专用炮仗、起火（起花）和烟盒花匣。从各种花炮烟火的名称看来，清朝的花炮已有多种花样，例如烟火杆子、线穿牡丹、水浇莲、金盘落月、飞天十响、五鬼闹判儿、炮打襄阳城等。可见，当时的烟花燃放都设定了一定的形式以及数量，它的复杂与奢华足以证明烟花在元宵节中的重要性。

六、
古代女子的狂欢节

中国古代对于女子有众多的约束，从身体上的裹小脚到思想上的"三从四德"都限制着女子们的生活。而在普天同庆的元宵节中，女子们就像获得了"解放"一样。锣鼓震天、灯火通明、歌舞升平的元宵节让平时很难出门的女子们有了狂欢的机会。因此，中国古代的元宵节中"男妇戏游"是特有的景观。

○赏灯是元宵节的主要习俗

人们用"月光如水"来形容元宵节中的月光，而元宵节中的女子便是"似水柔情"。在拥挤的元宵灯市中，月光、灯光和烟火映在女子笑盈盈的脸面上，成为节日中一道最为美丽的夜景。节日中载歌载舞的是那些妙龄的少女们，她们在花灯下与心仪的男子窃窃私语，在节日的气氛中敞开心扉。

除了京城，其他地方的女子们也在元宵节中有很多活动，例如在元宵节中相约去拜"姑娘神"。姑娘神在北方称为"厕姑"或"坑三姑"，南方则称为"紫姑"或"戚姑"。另外，女子还有在元宵节"转三桥"的风俗，明清时较为流行。不能经常出门的女子们在元宵节这一天可以上街观赏花灯，家中男子不能跟随，他们要在城里通过三座桥才能获得祝福。

对于古代"大门不出二门不迈"的女子们来说，元宵节还是未婚女子们寻找心仪对象、恋人们单独相处的良机，因此，也有人认为元宵节是中国最早的"情人节"。

一些中国传统戏剧中也记录了男女在元宵节中的爱情故事。明代福州经典戏剧《荔镜记》中讲述了这样一个故事："福建泉州人陈三在潮州的元宵灯会上与富家女子黄五娘邂逅，便互相爱慕。黄五娘的父亲是个势利的人，要把五娘嫁给富豪林大，五娘伤心欲绝。陈三知道这件事后，来到潮州，打扮成一个磨镜匠人，混入了黄府，五娘在绣楼投以荔枝和手帕示爱。陈三故意在磨镜的时候将镜摔破，借口赔宝镜，卖身为奴。后来陈三和五娘在丫鬟益春的帮助下私奔回了泉州。"

另外，川剧《春灯谜》中也有元宵节中发生的爱情故事：有才有德的书生宇文彦与四川节度使韦初中之女韦文凤于元宵夜赏灯、猜谜中互生爱慕，经历种种波折误会终于喜结良缘。

Chapter Two
The Development of the Lantern Festivall

In different dynasties in China, the Lantern Festival varies in terms of customs and time durations.

It lasted one day in the Han Dynasty(202 BC—220 AD), three days in the Tang Dynasty(618 AD—907 AD), and five days in the Song Dynasty(960 AD—1279 AD). While in the Ming Dynasty(1368 AD—1644 AD), the Spring Festival and the Lantern Festival were celebrated as a whole, and lantern display continued from the 8th day to the 17th day of the first lunar month; during the festivals, people enjoyed shopping in the day and lantern display in the evening. In the Qing Dynasty(1644 AD—1912 AD), the celebration lasted only three to five days but contained more colorful activities. In the Republic of China (1912 AD—1949 AD), Lantern Festival was officially shortened into three days which remained until now in many places of China while in some places the festival was only celebrated on the 15th day of the first lunar month.

The customs of Lantern Festival get diversified with the times. The lantern display originated from the Han Dynasty, and was widely accepted in the Tang Dynasty as a festival

custom both in imperial palaces, and among common people. Some big lantern structures were built in the Tang imperial palace such as lantern wheels, lantern towers and lantern trees. Other customs were also gradually added into the festival celebration. In the Tang and Song Dynasties, variety shows became a fashion. In the Ming and Qing Dynasties, lantern riddles, dances, and operas gained their popularity. Today, on such an important traditional festival in China, people in different places created more cultural activities with local characteristics, such as the dragon lantern show, the lion dance, the stilts-walking, row land boating, the yangko dance, and the taiping drum dance.

1. The Lantern Festival in the Sui Dynasty

The Lantern Festival took its shape in the Sui Dynasty. After Emperor Wen of Sui Dynasty (541 AD—604 AD) unified China, the political turmoil had been curbed and the society was back on track of development and prosperity. As a result, the Lantern Festival became a carnival of the year. In *Book of Sui*, an official Liu Yu described the Lantern Festival celebration, "On the 15th evening of the first lunar month every year, people swarm into the streets and lanes, with their friends or families, to enjoy the celebration. Drums are beaten loudly; lanterns are lit up; people wear masks of animals and dress in costumes; all the variety shows and acrobatics are performed."

The successor Emperor Yang (569 AD—618 AD) was indulged in costly life, and resumed the Lantern Festival celebration, and even took it as an opportunity to show the wealth of state. On the festival night, Yang held a grand party in the imperial palace to receive the guests and envoys from other states. He also ordered lantern displays and variety shows to be prepared in the streets for the common people. *Book of Sui* recorded the history, "The celebration is splendid enough. Every place is full of colorful lanterns, music and dances. There are over 30,000 performers and 18,000 music players. The stage is as long as 4 kilometers. Countless people enjoy themselves in the parade day and night." *Book of Sui* also recorded that on the Lantern Festival night of 610 AD Emperor Yang invited some envoys and businessmen from the Western Regions to Luoyang, the capital city, with the aim at showing off wealth and power of the Sui Dynasty. On the full-moon night, a big platform was built up for the variety shows and operas in the street out of the Duan Gate of the imperial palace. More than 18,000 musicians were playing instruments in a circle of 2,500 meters around the platform thus the music could be heard miles away. The whole capital city was decorated with lanterns so that the night was as bright as the day. And the celebration lasted for 15 days. Emperor Yang also ordered to redecorate the capital city with top materials. All the trees and grasses were encircled with silks; even green grocers' shops were required to use fine grass matting on the ground. All the common people were told to wear magnificent costumes when they went out to the streets, while those poor people who did not have decent clothes were not allowed to go out, or they would be put into prison. When the western envoys and businessmen passed by a restaurant, the landlord would invite them to a dinner totally for free, and boasted, "China is so wealthy that all the restaurants are free of charge." Those envoys and businessmen actually knew that it was a lie, and replied, "There are many poor people in the land of China who are still worried about clothing, why not make clothes for them with those silks on the trees?"

2. The Lantern Festival in the Tang Dynasty

In the Tang Dynasty, the lantern custom was developed into a big lantern fair. In the late period of the Tang Dynasty, the Lantern Festival became a national carnival. In the capital city Chang'an, curfew was carried out every night except the three days of Lantern Festival. Thus both royal members and common people had freedom to light up lanterns and enjoy lantern shows in the streets on the three Curfew-Releasing Nights. The avenues were crowded with carriages and pedestrians, all in great excitement. Emperor Xuanzong (reigning from 712AD—756 AD) built a huge lantern tower with 10 meters wide and 50 meters tall. The tower was covered with silk, at the top of which stood the images of rising dragon and leaping tigers. Gold, silver, jade and pearl ornaments were hung at the corner of eaves; they clanged pleasingly when a soft wind blew away. It was such a splendid brightness at night seen from a distance.

Lantern fair was greatly developed in the Tang Dynasty. The imperial court spent much money building lantern wheels, lantern trees and lantern towers, and designing innovative and splendid lanterns. Gradually the celebration grew in scale.

Besides the lantern fair, other activities like dances and operas also attracted many people. The dancing performers were usually some very beautiful maids skilled at singing and dancing, who would wear very costly chaplets and silk capes.

Another game was invented in the Tang Dynasty for the festival celebration, named hook-pulling, the original form of tug-of-war today. In ancient China, tug-of-war was not a competitive game but a way to pray for good harvest and desirable weather. A large-scale tug-of-war was held every year by the imperial court in order to show the strong power of the state to its people and envoys from other states.

3. The Lantern Festival in the Song Dynasty

Since 967 AD, the Lantern Festival holidays grew to 5 days, 2 days more than that in the Tang Dynasty, with a prolongation of the 17th and the 18th day of the month. Consequently, the celebration grew on a large scale. In the Song Dynasty, on the festival night, the emperor and all the ministers would have a banquet together for universal celebration. Emperor Huizong (reigning from 1100 to 1126 AD) and his concubines would go to the Bell Tower to enjoy the lantern display. He was very generous to bestow a cup of wine on each maid around the tower. It was said that a girl tried to hide the gold cup after she drank the bestowed wine. But she was discovered on the spot and was taken to Emperor Huizong. The girl hit on an idea in emergency and recited a poem, "The full moon is circled with colorful lanterns, and I walked out to the imperial gate with my husband. Indulged in the grand dancing and singing, I lost my way. Now it was too late for going home, but I was lucky to have the bestowed wine. Being afraid of punishment from my family on my lateness, I tried to keep the gold cup as an evidence to save me out of the trouble." Emperor Huizong found it very impressive and agreed to let her go home with the cup.

Since the holidays extended, the businessmen took the opportunities to sell all new types of lanterns catering to the needs of market. And the production and patterns of lanterns improved a lot compared with the Tang Dynasty. According to *Dream of the Eastern Capital* by scholar Meng Yuanlao in the Song Dynasty, the lantern hills in the Song imperial palace were decorated with handicrafts made of colored silk, such as Manjushiri riding a lion, Visvabhadra riding a white elephant. The craftsmen used pulley tackle system to produce dynamic effects, and the arms of Bodhisattva could wave around, and the fingers were so slim and lifelike. Before the Lantern Festival, many county magistrates would, one after another, offer the local distinguished lanterns to the imperial palace, just to please their emperor. The glass lanterns in five colors from Suzhou, the white jade lantern from Fuzhou and the frameless lantern from Xin'an were all novel and eye-catching. The biggest one is the glass lantern of five colors, with a diameter of over one meter; its top cover is drawn with vivid pictures of mountains,

Guessing Lantern Riddles

waters, people, flowers and feathers.

The 15th night of the first lunar month was the climax of the Lantern Festival. In the lantern fair, people were surrounded by lanterns, dances, music, and variety shows. All the wineshops and teahouses in the capital city were decorated with colored lanterns with a great din of drums and pipes. The patterns of lanterns were also various. Some featured legendary figures like Zhong Kui and three gods of blessing, fortune, and longevity; some featured fruits like peach, plum and grape, some others featured birds and animals, like deer and crane. Men and women, the young and the old, all in festival costumes, indulged themselves in festival banquets, or had fun with each other by a heating stove until the next morning.

Dancing parade is another important activity in Lantern Festival celebrations. The dancing parade usually lasted from the 1st day to the 16th day of the first lunar month. People in the parade wore different masks and costumes, and acted in an amusing way to make the audience laugh. The dancing parade developed with the times. Even today in many places of China, there are performing teams dressed as historical or legendary figures in public celebrations.

Lantern riddle was added into the celebrations in the early time of the Song Dynasty. Riddles were written on the lanterns for people to guess for fun when they watched the lantern show. Since it was as difficult to guess a riddle as to shoot a tiger, the riddle on the lantern was also named "Lantern Tiger". The game has been popular until today.

The celebrations were so colorful that women in the Song Dynasty who were usually not allowed to go out were extremely excited about the Lantern Festival. They would dress themselves up very well before going out. As a response to the bright and clear moonlight, the ladies would choose white dresses and distinguished headwear. As was recorded in documents, it was common on that night that some ladies in heavy dress missed their decorations in the crowd, and when they lit up a lantern to look for their belongings, they could easily find earrings and necklaces that were lost by others.

4. The Lantern Festival in the Ming Dynasty

In the Ming Dynasty, the celebrations of Lantern Festival grew into 10 days lasting from the 8th to the 17th day of the first lunar month, with the lantern fair as its main activity. In 1409 AD, Emperor Chengzu sent out an imperial decree that all the officials would have a 10-day holiday for the Lantern Festival which began from the 11th day of the first lunar month.

Different from other dynasties, it was very popular in the Ming Dynasty to observe three customs: bridge walking, nail touching and walking for health. The so-called bridge walking meant that on the 16th night of the first lunar month, all women in the city would walk over bridges with each other's support in a good wish to eliminate diseases. Thus the custom was also named walking-for-health, and those who could not cross the bridges were believed not to have a long lifespan. Secondly, nail-touching meant those who touched the bronze nail on the Qianmen Gate of Beijing, were blessed to give birth to a boy. The custom was very popular in the Qing Dynasty.

A painting titled "the Lantern Display of the Lantern Festival" vividly relived the grand celebration in the capital city of Jinling (today's Nanjing) of the Ming Dynasty. The painting depicts a streetscape at the north of Qinhuai River in the Ming Dynasty, and over 2,000 figures are distinct to each other in manners. In the painting, various colored lanterns are raised up at the street shops; people swarm to the streets to watch the variety shows, some with great concentration, some showing satisfying smiles,

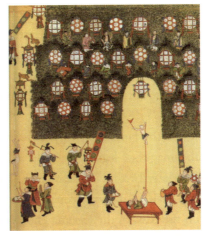

The Lantern Festival Carnival in the Reign of Ming Emperor Xianzong

and some others giving big applause; officials are followed by a bunch of servants while the common people just travel with two or three fellows; a lifelike dragon is composed of a series of lanterns; several little boys are lighting up firecrackers. The whole painting is very impressive.

5. The Lantern Festival in the Qing Dynasty

After the Manchu set up the Qing Dynasty, the Lantern Festival was shortened to 5 days, and the celebration duration in the palace was even shorter. According to imperial records, "All the officials have a three-day holiday from the 14th to the 16th day of the first lunar month." The emperor took this opportunity to hold a banquet in the palace to receive foreign guests, and prepared lantern shows and firework displays in an open area near the water in the Palace of Heavenly Purity or Yuanmingyuan Imperial Garden.

Ice lantern was another addition to the festival in the Qing

Dynasty. Since ice lantern can only be produced in winter, it is mainly popular in Northeast China. The Lantern Festival therefore had a new name Ice Lantern Festival. At present, the Harbin Ice Lantern Festival is best known in China, which lasts from the Spring Festival to the Lantern Festival for a period of time.

In the Forbidden City there was a special lantern hill with the image of a legendary turtle which originated from the Song Dynasty. In the Chinese legends, the turtle hill was a high mountain in the sea. People developed the design of lantern hill on the basis of the legend. The whole design took the shape of a big turtle carrying on its back a mountain with rocks, trees, lanterns and statues of gods. In the hill stood a performing stage for music bands and dances. The whole lantern hill was just like a fairyland with grand decorations and splendid lanterns. All the ministers felt it was an honor to watch the turtle lantern hill with the emperor.

Harbin Ice and snow world on the Lantern Festival

New development could be found in the civilian celebrations. There came out a novel lantern which could produce the sound of crickets. The crickets actually were hidden inside the lantern by the handicraftsmen before the festival. It was a great pleasure to watch lanterns and hear the chirp at the same time.

Lantern dance was another feature of Qing celebrations for the Lantern Festival. It was recorded that the number of dancers could be as many as 3,000, and each of them lifted a lantern and moved to the tune of *Song of Peace and Tranquility*. The 3,000 dancers formed a pattern of " 太 ", then changed into the form of another Chinese character " 平 ", and then " 万 " and " 岁 ", in the end they formed a final pattern of " 太平万岁 ", which means "Long Live the Peace and Tranquility". Fireworks display followed closely the lantern dance. The bangs of firecrackers, the clang of instruments and the laughers intertwined with each other under the bright flames. Dragon lantern dance was a common custom shared by the north and the south. Two dragon lanterns were held by a group of performers as the length of the dragon required. One performer was manipulating a dragon pearl to tempt the two dragons. The audiences cheered loudly as the dragons swiftly overturned in the air.

The firework display was a necessary accompaniment to the lantern show. In the Qing Dynasty, the variety of firecrackers had developed a lot which could be seen from the different names of firecrackers: Fireworks Pole, Thread Penetrating Peony, Water-Sprinkled Lotus, Golden Tray Flying to the Moon, Ten-bangs in the Sky, Five Kids Stirring up the Judge, and Artillery to Strike Xiangyang City. The quality

The Colorful Chinese Festivals
The Lantern Festival

and quantity of firework displays were stipulated. One may see the complexity and luxury of firework displays and their significance in the Lantern Festival celebration.

6. Women's Carnival in the Old Days

Chinese women in the old days were bound by many restrictions both physically and mentally, such as feet-binding custom, three obediences and four virtues. However in the national celebration for the Lantern Festival, women were given a total "freedom". The festival was just like a public carnival for all the Chinese women in the old days who seldom had the chance to go outside. Therefore, it was an unusual custom that men and women appeared in the same parade and performance for the festival celebration.

Chinese people often described the moonlight on the Lantern Festival as clear as water, and the women as gentle as water. In the crowded lantern fair, it was the most poetic

Watching Lanterns on the Lantern Festival

view to see that all the women's smiles were shone with the brightness of moonlight, lanterns and fireworks. Those young ladies might join in the dancers and singers, and it seemed a wonderful moment for them to open their hearts to their loved men under the colorful festival lanterns.

Women in other places also had lots of activities to enjoy, such as praying to Lady God, a prophet who was called "Toilet Lady" or "Three Goddesses of Toilet" in the north, and "Purple Goddess" or "Qi Goddess" in the south. In the Ming and Qing Dynasties, women also kept a custom called "three crossings of bridge". Interestingly, women on the Lantern Festival could go to the streets and cross three bridges for a good blessing, while their male family members were not allowed to follow.

For those single girls in the old society who stayed at home all year round, the Lantern Festival was a good time to meet and date with their Mr. Right, so the festival is also considered China's earliest Valentines' Day.

Some traditional Chinese operas also themed the romance. Fuzhou's classical opera *Leechee and Mirror* told us a story, "A Quanzhou man named Chen San encountered a girl Huang Wuniang on a lantern display in Chaozhou City. They fell in love with each other at the first sight, but Huang's father was so snobbish that he wanted to marry his daughter to a rich man. Huang cried hard but could do nothing. Chen heard the news and came to Chaozhou. He dressed himself up as a mirror grinder and came to Huang's residence. Huang recognized Chen and threw some leechee and her handkerchief off the tower to show her love for Chen. At such a sight, Chen decided to fight for his love. He broke a mirror on purpose and promised to do more manual work for Huang's father as compensation. Finally, with the help of a servant girl called Yichun, the two lovers found an opportunity and eloped successfully to Quanzhou."

A similar love story was depicted in a Sichuan Opera *Spring Lantern Riddles*: an intellectual Yu Wenyan met Wei Wenfeng, a daughter of an officer in Sichuan. They adored each other in a lantern riddle activity. Finally, they went into marriage after overcoming a lot of obstacles.

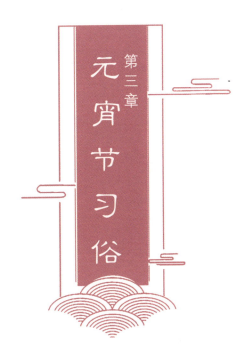

第三章

元宵节习俗

　　中国幅员辽阔，民族众多，不同地域呈现出不同的文化特征，节日习俗也不尽相同。就元宵节而言，节日文化自汉朝以来流传到中国的不同地方，具有普遍性的习俗有赏花灯、吃元宵、猜灯谜、放烟火等，而一些诸如走百病、迎紫姑、耍龙灯、"相偷"等习俗仅在一些地区流行。

多彩中国节

元宵节

　　所谓的"灯"，其实是灯笼，在中国古代既是照明的工具，也是元宵节中供赏玩的艺术品。中国人在赏灯的习俗中不断创新灯笼的样式，使其形状各具特色，因此，也被称为花灯。自汉代开始把正月十五月圆之夜作为节日以来，各个朝代的元宵节都与花灯有着密切的联系，形成了挂灯、赏灯、猜灯谜、对灯联、耍龙灯等众多与

〇各式各样的中国灯笼

灯相关的习俗。赏花灯是元宵节中最为重要的习俗,因此有些地方也把元宵节称为灯节。

(一)正月十五点灯

很久很久以前,在人间的凶禽猛兽很多。它们四处伤害人和牲畜,人们就组织起来消灭它们。一天,天帝的一只神鸟犯了错误,被贬下凡来,被一位不知情的猎人用弓箭射死了。

眼看神鸟受惩罚的期限已到,却不见它回到天庭。掌管人间生死的阎王爷禀报天帝神鸟被猎人射死的事情后,天帝勃然大怒,下令让天兵天将在正月十五到人间放火,把人间所有的一切通通烧毁。天帝有一个漂亮的女儿,心地非常善良,当她偷听到父亲下的命令后,不忍心看到人间无辜的百姓受到伤害。她冒着被父亲惩罚的危险偷偷下凡来到人间,把这个消息告诉了人们。大家对她的话半信半疑。射死神鸟的猎人出现了,他向百姓们坦白了射杀神鸟的事,人们开始慌张了。一些人开始把财产藏起来,寻找躲避的方法。一时间,整个人间处于恐慌之中。

一天,一位智慧的老人想出了一个办法,他说:"从正月十五开始接连三天,我们各家各户都点上灯笼,放鞭炮和烟火,这样的话,天帝就会误认为人间正在经历着大火。"大家认为老人的主意可行,便按照他的办法去准备灯笼、鞭炮和烟火。正月十五晚上,天帝在天门往人间一看,人间一片红光,响声震天,而且接下来的两天依然如此,天帝以为是燃烧的大火,心中甚是高兴。而人间的一切还是原来的样子,人们就这样保住了自己的性命及财产。人们为了纪念这次成功躲避劫难,从此每到正月十五,家家户户都要挂灯笼、放烟火。

（二）黄巢"挂灯护民"

黄巢（公元820年—884年）是唐代曹州人，是一个盐商。常年经商让他积累了很多的财富，另外，他还收留了很多亡命之徒。唐朝末年，民不聊生，特别是唐懿宗时期（860年—874年），皇室奢侈成风，赋税沉重，加上连年发生水、旱灾，人民的生活疾苦，出现了大量窃贼和土匪。

黄巢起兵反抗朝廷，攻打皇城三天三夜都不成功。眼看已到年关，将士们都非常疲惫了，他就下令撤兵，打算年后继续攻打。春节一过，黄巢孤身一人进皇城打探敌情，不小心被奸细发现，告诉了朝廷，朝廷便派兵满城搜查他。危难之时，一位老人救了他，并教了他攻打皇城的计谋。告别老人时，黄巢对他说："正月十五我会来攻城，我一定会成功的。请你告诉城里那些善良的老百姓们，正月十五那天在自己家门口点一个灯笼，我的军队进城后绝对不伤害点了灯笼的老百姓家。那些不挂灯笼的人家，就是贪官污吏，我们会全部杀掉。"

正月十五那天，黄巢的军队果然攻入了皇城，那些没点灯笼、欺压百姓的官吏们都被杀了。后来，人们为了纪念黄巢"护民除奸"的义举，便兴起了正月十五点灯笼的习俗。

二、
逛灯市

随着赏灯习俗的流行，中国不少地方形成了专门赏灯的灯市。灯市通常是在一些大城市中，特别是京城所在地。

（一）逛灯市的历史

唐朝时期，灯市已空前盛大。明朝节期的延长也让灯市更加热闹。明朝的元宵节还在河上放水灯，人们乘坐游船，边放灯边赏夜景。明成祖迁都北京（公元 1403 年）后，每逢上元节都要赐百官节假日，还在东华门设了灯市，专门在元宵节中挂灯。清朝各地的灯会各不相同。江南一带叫作上灯落灯，即十三日上灯，十八日落灯。清朝文献描述了这样的情景："十三夜，悬点灶灯于厨下，凡五夜，至十八夜止。"十三日夜通常家家要吃团子（汤圆），到了十八日落灯之夜，便要改换食面条了。在杭州一带，还要在十三日的前一日将灯节所引龙灯拿到龙神庙。四川一带的元宵节有灯山会。在四川西部，从正月初九"开灯"起，邻里相约，轮流设宴聚饮。初九这一餐叫"试灯宴"，每夜一家做东设宴，直至十六日。聚饮时，各家室内厅堂都必须挂灯亮盏，以示驱晦求吉。

○繁华的元宵节灯市

（二）花灯习俗

在古代，人们为了驱逐黑暗而点灯笼，灯笼象征着光明。随着历史的发展，各地元宵节挂花灯的习俗也具有了更多的象征意义。

元宵节中的挂灯有驱晦逐邪之意。清代，安徽、湖北一带要举行"照耗"仪式。照耗即有驱邪的意思。在江苏北部地区，元宵节的晚上要放火烧田，为的是烧死害虫及虫卵，以保证来年的丰收。在陕西一带，元宵夜流行"照黑角"，即家家户户要在家里各个角落挂上灯，使屋内灯火通明，另外还要挑着灯笼把房前、屋后、院中的所有黑暗角落全部照一遍，以示逐晦驱邪。

挂灯还透出人们祈福求平安的心愿。有一种灯叫作"光明灯"，通常挂在寺庙中，借佛的法力求得一年中平安顺利。也有农家在田间立长竹竿挂上一盏灯"照田蚕"，观察火色以预测一年的水旱情况，以期丰年。另外，也有放天灯的习俗。这一习俗起源于人们为了躲避盗匪侵袭而四散逃逸，以燃放天灯为互报平安的信号，灾难消除后，人们避难回家的日子是正月十五，以后人们便以放天灯的仪式来庆祝，所以又称天灯为"祈福灯"或"平安灯"。其后逐渐演变为向上天祈福许愿的民俗活动。天灯上写满了人们心里的各种祈愿，希望天灯能上达天庭，带给人无限的希望和光明。

○夜照田蚕

清朝元宵节中挂灯还与求子有关。在四川东部有"偷檐灯"之俗，偷灯者多为不孕妇女，或尚未得子人家。由于元宵节各家各户都要在房檐下挂灯，不孕妇女或无子人家的一人便会趁夜深人静时，偷偷溜到事先相中的一家（这家通常为子孙满堂），将这家檐下的灯偷至自家，以兆新年得子。在闽南语中，"灯"与"丁"发音相近，所以灯笼也用来求子添丁。

传说唐太宗李世民鼓励老百姓把孩子送去上学。开学的第一天，学生们要带一盏花灯到学校去，请博学的老先生点起来，这寓意着"前途光明"。而以前的私塾一般在正月十五后开学，学生们提着花灯去上学，似为元宵节的后续。

除了上述传统的象征意义之外，花灯在元宵节中最为重要的意义是"好看"。花灯各式各样的姿态让人目不暇接，灯光映衬着夜景为人们带来了更多的愉悦。

（三）花灯的种类

在中国，元宵节上的花灯种类繁多，形态千变万化，制作技艺也各具特色。在各式各样的中国花灯中，较为出名的灯有以下几种。

第一，宫灯，即古代皇宫或官府使用的灯。宫灯是中国花灯中最具特色的手工艺品，制作工艺精细，装饰精致，显示了皇家和大臣们的富贵和奢华。中国现存宫灯文物较早的有西汉时期的长信宫灯，这一宫灯形态为一梳髻的跣足侍女正坐在地，手持铜灯。灯的表面没有太多的修饰物和复杂的花纹，比较朴素。故宫博物院中收藏的最早的宫灯是明朝宫灯。

北京宫灯久负盛名，其中有一种绢画灯，具有强烈的宫廷色彩。"六方宫灯"是最具代表性的北京宫灯，分上宽下窄两层，上层六根短立柱头上雕龙、凤头，下层六根长立柱外侧有镂空花瓣。上、下层六柱间各镶一块画屏，所绘内容大都为吉祥如意、龙凤呈祥、福寿延年等。1915 年，

○北京宫灯

北京宫灯首次被送到巴拿马万国博览会展出，荣获金奖，受到国际好评。另外，从六方宫灯基础上发展而来的"花灯"在现代北京也很流行，选用红木、紫檀木、花梨木、楠木等贵重木材，加入了精细的雕刻技艺，品种有吊灯、壁灯、台灯、戳灯四种。北京宫灯的制作集木艺、雕刻、漆饰、编织、绘画等多种手工工艺于一身。制作一只灯要历经 100 多道工序，结构复杂的从开始备料到制作完成需要几个月时间。

河北藁城县屯头村被称为"宫灯之乡"。明代村里有一位姓李的师傅手工制作的纱灯非常精美耐用，官府豪门都喜欢挂他所制作的灯。据说到了清代，乾隆皇帝南巡看见这种灯，甚为喜欢，便让侍

从精选了一些带回皇宫。关于藁城的灯成为宫灯，还有这样一个传说：清代雍正年间，屯头村有一个老汉，心灵手巧，酷爱民间工艺，有一套做灯笼的手艺。每到年节，他都要做几对鲜艳夺目的灯笼挂在自家的门前，为新春佳节增添祥和、喜庆的气氛，每年都会吸引众街坊邻居围观欣赏。有一年，老汉做了几对灯笼到藁城集上来卖，恰巧被游集散心的县太爷看见了，便把所有灯笼都买下，挂在府邸整日观赏。灯笼做工别致，富丽堂皇，县太爷视为珍品，爱不释手。这年又到了向皇上进贡的日期，县太爷正苦思冥想送什么物品来取悦皇上，有人指点他送几对灯笼试试。县太爷虽有点舍不得，但为讨好皇上只得忍痛割爱。果然，皇上一眼看中，龙颜大悦，重赏了藁城知县。后来皇宫内外到处挂上了这大红的屯头灯笼。屯头灯笼由此被定为贡品，取名贡灯，成为皇宫专用品。后来人们把"贡"字换作"宫"字，就成了现在的"宫灯"。

第二，苏灯，又称姑苏灯彩，闻名于苏州。早在宋代，灯彩在苏州已成为独立的工艺行业。综合了绘画、剪纸、裱糊、纸扎、编织、刺绣、雕刻、泥人、绢人等工艺而制作出来的苏灯造型优美，色泽鲜艳，画面精致。与其他灯相比，苏灯的独特之处在于结合了苏州古典园林的建筑艺术和明代吴门画派的绘画艺术，形成了独特的风格：以亭台楼阁为造型主体，灯内配以人物、山水、花卉、鸟兽等彩色画面，集中体现了江南水乡的民间风味。在形形色色的彩灯中，走马灯最具巧思。它的外形是如碧瓦飞甍的亭台，灯壁有双层暗花，由于烛燃烧后引起空气对流，灯的内壁能自动转动，使灯上的人物故事走马似地循环往复展现在人们眼前，引人入胜。

第三，硖石灯。浙江海宁的硖石灯早在宋代就是贡品，其特点在于针刺工艺，采用竹篾为骨架造型，糊纸绘图，完全是手工针刺花纹。

另外，我国著名的民间元宵花灯还有南京夫子庙莲花灯、青海湟源排灯、泉州花灯、温州珠灯、上海金鱼壁灯等，无不令人叹为观止。一些地方的人家还会用面团做成各种形状的灯，如碗灯、上粗下细中间有碗的倒挂金钟灯、形如酒杯的酒盅灯、形似花瓶的瓶灯，等等。做好后放在蒸笼里蒸熟，出锅冷却后将灯中倒入豆油，放上灯捻，到用时点燃。为了使灯具有不同的颜色，人们使用不同的面粉来制作，用玉米面做成的灯金光闪闪，叫"金灯"；用小麦面粉做成的灯白盈盈的洁净，叫"银灯"；用荞麦面做的灯黑黝黝的结实，叫"铁灯"；用彩纸糊成的各种灯，灯中放小蜡烛，五彩缤纷，非常好看；还有用玻璃片拼成的玻璃灯，在玻璃面上贴上各种彩色人物花鸟剪纸，蜡烛光一照，极富美感。

○在南京秦淮风光带举行的 2012 年江苏秦淮灯会

南京夫子庙

　　南京夫子庙，即南京孔庙、南京文庙，位于南京市秦淮区秦淮河北岸贡院街，江南贡院以西，为供奉祭祀孔子之地，是中国四大文庙之一，为中国古代江南文化枢纽之地、金陵历史人文荟萃之地，不仅是明清时期南京的文教中心，同时也是居东南各省之冠的文教建筑群，现为夫子庙秦淮风光带重要组成部分。

　　夫子庙是一组规模宏大的古建筑群，主要由孔庙、学宫、贡院三大建筑群组成，占地极大。有照壁、泮池、牌坊、聚星亭、魁星阁、棂星门、大成殿、明德堂、尊经阁等建筑。夫子庙被誉为秦淮名胜而成为古都南京的特色景观区，是中国最大的传统古街市，与上海城隍庙、苏州玄妙观和北京天桥为中国四大闹市。

　　交通：

　　1）从南京禄口乘坐机场大巴城西线至中华门下，换乘地铁一号线至三山街站下，大约一小时到达夫子庙；或乘坐机场轻轨至终点站南京南站下，换乘地铁一号线同样到三山街站下，大约五十分钟至一小时至夫子庙。

　　2）从南京火车站乘坐公交车至夫子庙站下即达，或在火车站乘坐地铁（1号线）到三山街站下，出地铁3号出口向东一直走就可到达夫子庙。

　　现代的元宵节中，除了可以欣赏到传统花灯，还可欣赏到加入了现代技术的声控、光控、磁控和电子遥控等新型灯彩。如声控灯，只要观赏者为之鼓掌，便会自动亮光。

三、
吃元宵

　　元宵是中国的传统美食，也是元宵节中必不可少的食物。元宵之夜是月圆之夜，也是合家团圆之日，因此元宵的形状被做成圆形。圆在中国文化中代表着和美、包容、圆满，也象征着团结。

　　元宵节吃元宵的习俗源于宋朝，那时元宵被叫作汤圆。"圆子、团子、元子、水团、汤团"等食品名称，即是宋朝人对元宵的称呼。从有关记载看，当时元宵的种类已经很多了。元朝《武林旧事》中所记载的"节食所尚，则乳糖圆子、科斗粉、豉汤"，说的是元宵节街上售卖的节令食品。明朝之后，元宵的制作越来越讲究，明朝刘若愚在《酌中志》中记载了元宵的做法：用糯米细面，内用核桃仁、白糖为馅，沥水滚成，如核桃大，即江南所

○元宵

称汤圆。其与今天制作方法已经非常相似。

　　元宵节中吃元宵成为中国人流传至今的习俗。如果正月十五这天没有吃元宵，就不能算是完整地过了年。吃了元宵之后，元宵节团团圆圆的寓意便得到了升华。

　　作为食物，中国的元宵包含着很多文化。各地的元宵特色和制作方法各不相同，表现了各不相同的地域饮食文化。

　　总的来看，元宵的主材料有糯米面、高粱面、黄米面、苞谷面或紫米面。从种类上分，可分实心和带馅的两种。带馅的又有甜、咸之分。甜馅一般有猪油豆沙、白糖芝麻、桂花什锦、枣泥、果仁、麻蓉、杏仁、白果、山楂等；咸馅一般有鲜肉丁、火腿丁、虾米等。用芥、葱、蒜、韭、姜组成的菜馅元宵，称"五味元宵"，寓意勤劳、长久、向上。元宵的吃法也很多，可水煮、炒、油炸、蒸等。煮元宵时可加入酒酿、白糖、桂花等，吃上去别有一番风味。元宵的制作方法南北各异。北方的元宵多用箩滚手摇的方法，南方的汤圆则多用手心揉团。元

○彩色汤圆

宵可以大似核桃、也有小似黄豆。

　　元宵节为什么要吃汤圆，以及汤圆与元宵的名称由来，民间流传着这样一些故事。

（一）楚昭王与元宵

　　春秋末年，楚昭王（约公元前 523 年—前 489 年）在归家途中发现江中漂浮着一白色球状物，船工捞起后献给他。昭王剖开后见其瓣红如胭脂，香味扑鼻，他吃后，感到味道甘美。便问左右大臣这是什

○酒酿汤圆

么东西，大臣中没有一个人知道。昭王心中就不高兴了，于是派人去向孔子请教。孔子说："这种东西叫浮萍果，您得到它，是大王复兴的好兆。"此时正值元古月望，即正月十五，楚昭王心中大喜，便令人每年这天用面粉仿制这种果煮熟后食用，以图圆满吉祥。从此，正月十五吃元宵便流传至今。

（二）嫦娥与汤圆

　　元朝有这样一个故事：嫦娥抛下后羿奔月之后，后羿每夜苦苦思念她，终成重病。有一年正月十四日的夜晚，忽然来了一名童子求见。原来童子是嫦娥派来的信使，他告诉后羿：夫人也很思念你，但已上天成仙，无法下降。等到明天月圆的时候，请你用米粉做成丸子，团团如月，放在房屋的西北方向，呼叫夫人的名字。到夜半之后，夫人就可以从天而降。后羿按照童子的说法，做了圆圆的糖丸子放在房子西北角，心情急切地等待着嫦娥的到来。三更时分，嫦娥果

○嫦娥

然飘香下凡，与后羿见面，两人互吐了思念之情。从此之后，人们便把汤圆被视为祈求团圆的食物，每到正月十五，人们都要吃汤圆，寄寓团圆之意，憧憬美好人生。

（三）袁世凯与元宵

传说，1911 年辛亥革命后，袁世凯（公元 1859 年—1916 年）经南北议和，合法就任首任大总统。袁世凯篡夺了辛亥革命成果后，一心想复辟登基当皇帝，又怕人民反对，终日提心吊胆。一天，他听到街上卖元宵的人拉长了嗓子在喊："元宵。"觉得"元宵"两字与"袁消"谐音，有袁世凯被消灭之嫌。联想到自己的命运，于是在 1913 年元宵节前，下令禁止称"元宵"，只能称"汤圆"或"粉果"。然而，"元宵"两字并没有因他的意志而取消，元宵的说法依然在民间流传。

四、猜灯谜

猜谜最早出现在春秋时期（公元前 770 年—公元前 476 年），被称为"隐语"。猜灯谜是围绕元宵花灯而进行的娱乐活动，宋朝才开始流行，有的地方也叫"打灯谜"。人们把谜语写在纸上，然后贴在花灯上让其他人猜。关于元宵节中猜灯谜的习俗，民间流传着这样一个故事。

相传，很早以前，有个姓胡的财主，家产万贯，横行乡里，看

○ 猜灯谜

人行事，皮笑肉不笑，人们都叫他"笑面虎"。这"笑面虎"最爱以貌取人，只要是比自己穿得好的，他就拼命巴结，曲意逢迎；而对那些破衣烂衫的穷人，他就横眉竖眼，就像凶神恶煞一样。

有一年，春节快要到了，胡家门前一前一后来了两个人。前边的名叫李才，穿得衣帽整齐，颜色鲜艳，后边的叫王少，穿得破破烂烂。家人一见李才，忙去禀报。"笑面虎"慌忙迎出门来，一见来客衣帽华丽，忙露出满面笑容，恭敬相让。李才骄横地说："借给我十两白银。""笑面虎"忙让人取过银两，拱手相送。李才接过银子，扬长而去。

"笑面虎"还没回过神来，王少赶忙走上前去说："老爷，家里断粮了，请你借给我一斗粮食吧。""笑面虎"转过身来，瞟了一眼王少，见是一个衣着破烂的穷汉，就暴跳如雷地骂道："你这穷小子，给我滚！"王少还没来得及争辩，就被家丁赶走了。

回家的路上，王少越想越生气。猛然心生一计，要斗斗这个"笑面虎"。转眼间，春节过去了，元宵节就要到来了。各家各户都在忙着做花灯，王少也乐哈哈地忙了一天。到了元宵节晚上，家家户户都在门头房前挂上了各式各样的花灯。王少也打着一盏花灯上了街。他的花灯又大又亮，更为特别的是上面还题着一首诗。

王少来到"笑面虎"门前，把花灯挑得高高的，引来好多人观看。"笑面虎"正在门前观灯，一见此情景，连忙挤到花灯前看了起来。花灯上的诗句，"笑面虎"认不全，更念不通，就让身后账房先生给他念。账房先生摇头晃脑地念道："头尖身细白如银，论秤没有半毫分。眼睛长到屁股上，光认衣裳不认人。"

"笑面虎"一听，气得暴眼圆睁，脸色像涨紫了的茄子，哇哇乱叫："好小子，胆敢来骂老爷！"接着，就命家丁来抢花灯。王少忙挑起花灯，笑嘻嘻地说："老爷，怎么见得是骂你呢？""笑面虎"气哼哼地说："你那灯上是怎么写的？"王少又朗声念了一遍。"笑面虎"

恨恨地说道："这不是骂我光认衣服不认人吗？"王少仍笑嘻嘻地说："噢，老爷是犯了猜疑，自找挨骂。我这首诗是个谜语，谜底就是'针'。你想想，是不是？""笑面虎"一想，可不是吗，只气得面红耳赤，干瞪眼，什么话也说不出来，转过身去，狼狈地溜走了。周围的人都乐得哈哈大笑。

　　王少制作灯谜嘲弄老财的事，第二天就传开了，越传越远。从那以后，人们便开始在元宵花灯上写灯谜，供游人猜测，猜中有奖，谓之"元宵节射灯虎"。以后相沿成习，每逢元宵灯节各地都举行"灯谜"活动，一直传到现在。

　　猜灯谜被认为是元宵节中一个智慧的游戏，灯谜利用的是汉语字词多义的特点，被猜出的灯谜的答案通常不是谜语字面上表达的意思。如今每逢元宵，各个地方都打出灯谜，既增添了节日的乐趣，也希望来年能喜气洋洋、平平安安。

○猜灯谜

五、
对灯联

对联是中国的文化瑰宝之一，俗称对子。对联是写在纸、布上或刻在竹子、木头上的对偶语句，言简意深，对仗工整，平仄协调，是一字一音的中文语言独特的艺术形式。完整的对联需要有上联和下联，节日中的对联往往还要加入具有画龙点睛作用的横批。

灯联是贴在花灯上或用于灯会中的对联，通常包括上联和下联。人们在大门上或显眼的柱子上镶挂壁灯联、门灯联，也有文人墨客们喜欢在花灯上做出一个上联，让其他赏灯的人对出下联。在古代元宵节中，一边喝酒，一边赏灯、对灯联是一件非常惬意的事情。

历史上还流传着北宋著名政治家王安石（公元1021年—1086年）对灯联的故事。传说王安石20岁那年赴京赶考，元宵节那日他路过一个城市，被美景所吸引，便边走边赏灯。巧遇一个大户人家高悬走马灯，灯下悬一则上联，征对招亲。联是这样写的："走马灯，灯走马，灯熄马停步。"王安石读后，一时未能对出，便默默记在心中。到了京城，说来也巧，考题正好是："飞虎旗，旗飞虎，旗卷虎藏身。"王安石即以招亲联对出，并被取为进士。返乡途中，当王安石再次路过那户人家时，听说那招亲联仍无人对出，他便又以主考官的出联回对，结果被招为乘龙快婿。

清朝时，安徽桐城有一对父子宰相，父亲叫张英，儿子叫张廷玉，被称为"父子双学士，老小二宰相"。有一年元宵佳节，张府照例张灯结彩，燃放鞭炮。老宰相出联试子："高烧红烛映长天，亮光铺满地。"小廷玉思索时听到门外一声花炮响，顿时有了主意，对道："低点花炮震大地，响气吐冲天。"对仗工整，天衣无缝，堪称绝妙。

清朝时的浙江吴兴人闵鹗元自幼擅长对联，常常是出口成联。有一年元宵节，他随父亲到毛尚书家做客。夜晚恰逢乌云遮月，星光暗淡，一位客人应景出了一个上联："元宵不见月，点几盏灯为山河生色。"对联一出，所有的宾客陷入冥思苦想中，过了许久，都没人对出下联。一旁玩耍的闵鹗元听得鼓声阵阵，不禁文思涌动，随口吟出一则下联："惊蛰未闻雷，击数声鼓代天地宣威。"客人们听闻这一下联，无不拍案叫绝。

六、
赏灯诗

历代的文人在元宵节中创作了大量与元宵节相关的美妙诗词，流传至今。为了重温当年诗句中所描述的美景，现代的人们在元宵节中便把这些古诗句写在花灯上，让人们欣赏。灯诗的内容涉及元

宵节的各个方面，有描
述景色的，如唐朝诗人
郭利贞的《上元》，诗曰：
"九陌连灯影，千门遥月
华。倾城出宝骑，匝路转
香车。烂漫惟愁晓，周
游不问家。更逢清管发，

○赏灯诗

处处落梅花。"也有一些灯诗描述的是元宵节中作者的情感，如北宋
词人秦观的《蝶恋花》写道："今岁元宵明月好，想见家山，车马应
填道。路远梦魂飞不到。清光千里空相照。"诗中透露了作者在元宵
节在外远游，由于孤独寂寞而想象家乡热闹的节日景象，流露出渴望
与家人团聚的思乡之情。

七、耍龙灯

中华民族崇尚龙，把龙作为吉祥的象征。耍龙灯，也称舞龙灯
或龙舞，起源可以追溯到上古时代。传说，早在黄帝时期，在一种
名为《清角》的大型歌舞中，就出现过由人扮演的龙头鸟身的形象，
其后又编排了六条蛟龙互相穿插的舞蹈场面。见于文字记载的龙舞，

是汉代张衡的《西京赋》，作者在百戏的铺叙中对龙舞作了生动的描绘。

在古代人的观点中，龙是神物，能够呼风唤雨，消灾解难。在重要的节庆中祭拜龙，是为了祈求风调雨顺，元宵节中的舞龙习俗也就源于此。宋代吴自牧在《梦粱录》中记载：正月十五元夕节时，有用草编成的龙，上面布置着灯烛，远看蜿蜒盘旋，像双龙要飞走一样。可见当时的龙是用草编而成，后来则用各种材料所做成。龙灯普遍用篾竹扎成，前有龙头，身体中间节数不等，但一般为单数，每节下面有一根棍子以便撑举。每节内燃蜡烛的就称为"龙灯"。耍龙灯的表演，有"单龙戏珠"与"双龙戏珠"两种。耍龙灯时，由一人持彩珠戏龙，龙头随珠转动，其他许多人各举一节相随，上下掀动，左右翻舞，并以锣鼓相配合，甚为壮观。

○龙灯

八、放烟火

在中国一些重要的节日中，放烟花是一个非常重要的仪式。除夕夜放烟火表示辞旧迎新，元宵夜则表示年节结束。

中国放烟花的历史久远，烟花的技艺非常成熟，式样也繁多。最著名的是花盒，每当夜晚在月下燃放时，盒中的人物、花鸟等五彩缤纷的烟火图像都很清晰，在空中如同挂画。晚清时期的一种御

○元宵节放烟火

073

用花盒叫"烟火城"，造型为小型城池，有城楼四门和雉堞刁斗旗杆及桥梁等物，并有守城兵丁。点燃后，城墙上齐放光明，烟花灯火一齐发作，桥梁落下，现出满桥莲花。一种名叫"八角美人亭"的烟火点燃后，亭角珠灯齐明，亭中美人动作如真人。"花牌楼"烟火，在大牌楼下排列"狮、象、虎、豹"，额嵌"万寿无疆"，点燃后，象身宝瓶随之放出，高及四五丈，各兽有的吐焰，有的射花筒，兽眼皆放射莲花，焰火尽时，百兽跪伏在地，做成百兽庆寿状。

现今中国的元宵节，有些地方政府会统一在一个地方放烟火供大家观赏，因每只烟火的燃放需要几分钟，燃放完所有的烟火通常要持续很长时间。普通人家会自己购买烟火，多为小型烟火，全家人一起欣赏。

九、
踩高跷

在元宵节的集体娱乐活动中，有踩高跷的表演。踩高跷也称"高跷""踏高跷""扎高脚""走高腿"，是中国民间盛行的一种群众性技艺表演。据说踩高跷是古代人为了采集树上的野果为食，在自己的腿上绑两根长棍，之后便发展成为一种跷技活动。古代的高跷都是木制的，在刨好的木棒中部做一支撑点放脚，然后再用绳索缚于腿

○踩高跷

部。踩高跷属中国古代百戏中的一种，早在春秋时已经出现。

关于踩高跷的起源，民间有不同的传说。春秋战国时期，历任齐国齐灵公、齐庄公、齐景公三朝卿相的晏婴的故事最为盛行。一次，晏婴出使邻国，因为其身材矮小，被邻国的大臣们耻笑。他很生气，就装一双木腿，顿时高大起来，这一举措弄得邻国国君臣子们啼笑皆非。看到这一情形，他更生气了，便借题发挥，运用他的滑稽挖苦那些大臣，使他们更狼狈。后来，踩高跷流传到了民间，成为一种娱乐活动。

另外还有一个把踩高跷与贪官污吏相联系的传说。从前，有座县城叫两金城，城里和城外的人民非常友好，每年元宵节都联合办社火，互祝生意兴隆、五谷丰登。后来，两金城来了个贪官，把社火看作是一个发财的机会，他便规定，凡是进出城办社火者，每人都要要交三钱银。城里城外的人们对这一规定非常不满，没有一个人愿意在进出城门时候交费。这个贪官命令手下关了城门，把护城河上的吊桥拉起来。城外的人非常聪明，他们便创造了高跷，即使城门关了，吊桥被拉起来了，他们也能踩着高跷过护城河、翻越城墙，到城里过节。这个贪官无奈只好放弃了他的生财之道，而踩高跷却成为一个节日习俗流传下来。

现代的高跷变化不大，但表演者需要穿着戏装。高跷又分高跷、中跷和跑跷三种，最高者有3米多。表演者踩着高跷，还要做各种动作，如舞剑、劈叉、跳凳、过桌子、扭秧歌等。现在元宵节中的踩高跷的表演者，扮演的多是戏曲中的角色，如关公、张飞、吕洞宾、何仙姑、张生、红娘、济公等。他们踩着高跷边演边唱，如履平地，还要不时做出滑稽的动作逗乐观众。

十、舞狮子

"舞狮子"又称"狮子舞""太平乐"。传说，狮子并不是中原之物，而是汉武帝派张骞出使西域后，和孔雀等一同带回的贡品。也有人说，狮子是文殊菩萨的坐骑，它的图像是随着西域的佛教传入中国的。而舞狮的技艺源于西凉（今甘肃西部酒泉、敦煌一带）的假面戏。

中国传统民俗认为舞狮可以驱邪避鬼。每逢元宵佳节或集会庆典，民间都以舞狮前来助兴。一般认为，舞狮习俗起源于三国时期，南北朝时开始流行，兴盛于唐朝。如今，舞狮一般由三人完成，二人装扮成狮子（其中一人充当狮头，一人充当狮身和后脚），另一人当引狮人。舞法上又有文武之分，文舞表现狮子的温驯，有抖毛、打滚等动作，武舞表现狮子的凶猛，有腾跃、蹬高、滚彩球等动作。现今，中国很多地方的元宵节中都要进行舞狮子表演。

○ 双狮共舞

十一、荡秋千

　　早在远古时代，人们为了获得高处的食物，在攀登中创造了荡秋千的活动，最早称为"千秋"，传说为中国北方的山戎族所创。开始仅是一根绳子，双手抓绳而荡。春秋时期齐桓公北征山戎族，把"千秋"带入中原。至汉武帝时，宫中以"千秋"为祝寿之词，取"千秋万寿"之意，以后为避忌讳，将"千秋"两字倒转为"秋千"。以后逐渐演化成用两根绳加踏板的秋千，因其设备简单，容易学习，深受人们的喜爱，很快在各地流行起来。汉代以后，秋千逐渐成为元宵、端午等节日进行的民间体育活动并流传至今。

○ 清代绘本《月曼清游图》中荡秋千场景

　　现在，每年元宵节期间，河北省的武安、涉县、磁县一带的城乡群众有荡秋千的习惯。一过正月初十，人们就开始在村街口开阔处和自家院内搭起高低不同的秋千架。从搭成到正月十六，每天都要荡一阵子，其中十四、十五两天是高潮。人们认为，荡秋千能祛除疾病，这也许就是荡秋千能世代相传、经久不衰的原因。连不会走路的孩子和年过古稀的老人，也要在别人的扶持下荡上几下。荡秋千分单人荡、双人荡、立荡、坐荡，等等。河北的许多村镇都有自己的秋千高手，有时还要举行表演比赛，荡得最高最美的人很受乡邻的赞扬。荡秋千的这些日子，也常常是青年男女相遇、接触的好机会。

十二、逐鼠

魏晋时期，元宵节开始流行一种逐鼠的活动，这一习俗一直盛行于古代南方盛产桑蚕的广大地区。冬天刚过、立春不久的正月十五，农户田里家里的老鼠开始活动，但这时它们行动迟缓，正是消灭老鼠的好时机。老鼠通常被认为是害物，但古代人认为老鼠是五谷神，不敢轻易消除，但又担忧老鼠在夜里把蚕吃掉，只能讨好它。于是就在元宵节这天煮一锅肉粥，放在老鼠时常出没的地方，一边放一边嘴里还念念有词，诅咒老鼠吃了肉粥后再祸害蚕就不得好死。

关于用粥祭祀以求蚕桑丰收，有这样一个故事：很久很久以前，有个叫吴县的地方有一个叫张成的人，他起夜时看到一个美丽的姑娘站在他家院子的东南角，向他招手呼唤。张成走上前去，姑娘便对他说："我是你们家这个地方的神，明年正月十五的时候，你做好粥，上面盖上肉来祭祀我。你们家的蚕桑就能丰收。"说完后，姑娘突然消失了。第二年元宵节，张成按照那位仙姑的说法，做了粥祭祀，结果那一年他们家的蚕获得了大丰收。从此以后他每年都这样做，果然年年都丰收。

有些地方还有元宵节照鼠耗的逐鼠风俗。在湖南宁乡，元宵节晚上人们以香蘸茶油，点燃后插于屋内各个角落，使老鼠不敢出洞耗粮毁物；有的地方还边插香边念咒语，把"客虫"（老鼠）驱逐出屋。

十三、
送灯

元宵节中送灯的习俗，大体上分为两种，一种是父母送给女儿的灯，一种是送给神灵的灯。

在汉语中，"灯"与"丁"谐音。在有些地方，元宵节前，娘家送花灯给新嫁女儿家，或一般亲友送给新婚不育之家，以求添丁吉兆。女儿出嫁后的第一个年头，农历正月初八到正月十五期间，娘家要送花灯给女儿女婿，一般送大宫灯一对；如果女儿已怀孕，还要送小灯笼两对，并配上点到落灯时的蜡烛。这种送灯又叫送"孩儿灯"，祝愿女儿孕期平安。送灯习俗在各地有所不同，寓意也稍有差异，但主要还是围绕着"求子"的愿望。

○海南文昌元宵送灯

　　元宵节这一天，一些农村要用灯祭祀神灵。他们成群结队地拿着花灯，一路上敲锣打鼓，放着鞭炮，把灯挂到村子里的庙宇中。挂好之后，人们便上去抢灯，据说谁家抢到，就喻示着来年会发财，人丁兴旺。也有的地方元宵节要做很多盏灯，在日落之前就要点灯，先把灯送到祖先牌位前，为了祈求祖宗显灵，保佑家人出入平安、生活幸福。然后再送灯到天地、灶神的牌位上，以求神仙赐福家人。又送到仓库、牛马圈、井台、碾坊等处，以求五谷满仓、牛肥马壮，打水平安、粮食常吃常有。再送到大路口，祈求出入平安，家来四面八方客。最后由每家的长房长子用筐挎着面灯和别的灯送到祖坟上。往祖坟送灯时，见到熟人不能说话，只能点头示意，以示祭奠祖宗的严肃。到坟前点灯时，不能借火柴用，否则意味着自家的日子过不起来，日子不红火。给祖坟送灯如果使用蜡烛，则必须是红色或黄绿色的蜡烛，忌讳点白色蜡烛。因为白色蜡烛叫"大白杆"，忌点白色蜡烛是为了避免下辈子有"光棍"之灾。坟前一般送金银灯，让祖宗在阴间金银常有、荣华富贵。将坟前金银灯放好后，用事先带好的油拌谷糠，将祖坟围成四方形，西南角留一缺口为门，在门口放一盏铁灯。这时，在上风口将油谷糠点燃，立时形成一条火龙，俗称火龙灯，意为祖坟有龙围绕、守护，风水好，吉利。最后将门口的铁灯点燃，为祖宗灵魂上西天大路照路。送灯人点燃铁灯后磕头、念祝词，然后离开坟地回家。

○ 满街的红灯笼

在海南文昌，元宵节送灯是一项传统。到了农历正月十五夜晚，人们掌着一盏盏花灯。灯上有 72 个大小红"喜"字，36 个"寿"字，还印有"招财进宝""连生贵子"等吉利的词或思古幽情的人物风景画。由一个"灯主"领队，排成长龙，敲锣打鼓，燃放爆竹沿村游行，然后到离村不远的公庙去。花灯挂在庙的内外，灯一挂好，人们便蜂拥而上去抢采花灯，据说，抢到了花灯便能发财、人丁兴旺。关于"灯主"的产生，还有一番讲究。在文昌本地方言中，"灯"与人丁的"丁"谐音，人们便把"灯"和"丁"联系起来，送灯有人丁兴旺的意思，所以"灯主"由村中有男孩、家景兴旺的村民轮流当。主要负责筹备资金、联系演戏、跳舞、祭公、送公灯等事项。参加送灯的人家也必须是生有男孩的家庭。元宵节中除送灯外，还有跳盅盘舞、演木偶戏、琼戏等文娱活动。

十四、
迎紫姑

十四、迎紫姑

紫姑是中国民间的一个神。关于紫姑神的来历，有不同的说法。有说紫姑未成为神之前是一户人家的婢妾，因遭家里其他夫人的嫉恨，便让她干脏活，折磨她。紫姑不堪虐待，于正月十五那天激愤而死。另一说法出自《封神演义》中云霄、琼霄、紫霄三位仙姑摆黄河阵的故事。这三位仙姑的哥哥赵公明（后来被封为财神爷）应闻太师的请求，帮助殷纣王打西岐的周国，后来被陆压道人施法术弄死。三位仙姑为兄报仇，摆下了黄河阵，用混元金斗这件法宝，把元始天尊十二弟子的大部分打进了黄河阵。后来元始天尊和老子大施法力，破了黄河阵，三位仙姑也随即丧命。姜子牙封神时，因为她们使用的法宝混元金斗就是马桶，所以封三位仙姑为坑三姑娘，即厕神。还有一种说法，说紫姑，姓何名媚，寿阳刺史李景害死了她的丈夫并把她纳为侍妾，引起李景大老婆的妒恨。正月十五元宵节夜里，大老婆将何媚杀害在厕所中。何媚冤魂不散，李景上厕所时，常听到她的啼哭声。天帝知道此事，非常可怜何媚，便封她为厕所之神。

　　各地迎紫姑的目的各有不同，但基本上与扶乩和蚕桑业相关。对于扶乩，一般在厕所或猪栏边进行，有的人家用旧衣服包在扫帚上或用玉米秆、稻草扎成假人，并糊以五颜六色的彩纸，用葫芦瓢等画成紫姑的头脸。迎紫姑时要念咒语："子胥（其夫）不在，曹夫人（大妇）已行，小姑可出嬉。"如果扫帚变重，表示紫姑神降临，就可以向紫姑卜问能以数字回答的问题了，据说扫帚会点头作答。有的地方则不以扫帚等扎紫姑神，而是"提猪觉重者，则是神来，可占众事。"

　　在江浙一带蚕桑业发达的地方，把祭祀蚕神与拜迎紫姑的习俗联系在一起，通过接请紫姑，占卜新年蚕事。

十五、
走百病

　　明清时期，北京等地的正月十五有"走百病"的习俗。正月十五晚上，妇女们相约到外面，一人拿着香走在最前头引导其他人随行，有时顺着墙边走，有时通过桥，有时还要走到郊外去，这样认为可祛病延年，这种习俗被称为"走百病"，也叫"游百病"，"散百病"等，是一种消灾祈健康的活动。有的地方，除了"走百病"，还要"摸门钉"。因"钉"与"丁"谐音，而"丁"又象征男子。因此，妇女们会到各城门或寺庙去"摸门钉"，需要在黑暗中摸索，不得有照明设备，一次就摸中的人视为有生子的吉兆。现在元宵节的走百病习俗不仅仅是妇女，老人、小孩或体弱多病者也参与到走百病中来。

十六、
愉悦的"相偷"

古代的元宵节中还有一个有趣的习俗——偷菜，所以在一些地区，元宵节又有"偷放节"之称。据说，元宵节偷盗的习俗源于辽金时期，人们可以肆无忌惮地偷窃，官府不逮捕也不惩罚，而在其他时候，偷窃会被判很重的罪。

写于明崇祯八年（公元 1635 年）的《帝京景物略》中，作者提到金元时期元夕"三日放偷"的习俗。南北朝的契丹族于正月十三日、十四日、十五日夜连续三天"放偷"，女真族则于十六日夜"相偷"，即互相随便偷窃。相偷的传统从魏、齐流传到隋朝，且越来越热闹，其后的朝代也遗留了一些相偷的习俗。偷盗的人不是真的偷，是为了获得一种彩头，而被偷的人家也不会因为被偷而难过。大家你偷我的，我偷你的，纯粹是为了娱乐玩耍。

宋代洪皓的《松漠纪闻》中记载：在元宵节放偷习俗影响下，甚至是一些富人家的妇女也会在带着自家的婢女到别人家

○元宵节给神灵送灯

做客时，明目张胆地在主人迎客之时进行偷窃。若是被主人家发现，只需送一些茶和糕点上门，便可了事。不同地区元宵节放偷的习俗中，偷的东西各不相同。有偷灯的，也有偷菜的。偷灯与送灯的习俗很早就有，其意义相同，都是祝愿得子的意思。宋朝时期，有的人认为正月十五日的灯可以使人生子，若夫妇共同去别人家偷来，放置床下，当月可怀孕。民间还流传着这样的谣唱："偷了刘家的灯，当年吃了当年生，有了女孩叫灯哥，有了男孩叫灯成。"有些地区的人家在元宵节会做一些用豆面捏成或用萝卜雕刻成的花灯，那些婚后想要孩子的妇女们就会到别人的家门口偷灯吃，且一般还要偷姓氏为"刘"或"戴"的人家，因为取其谐音，有"留住孩子""带来孩子"的意思。

偷菜的习俗在现代中国的一些地方还保留着。在台湾的一些地区，未婚女性会在元宵节中偷洋葱或其他蔬菜，以祈求能够嫁个好丈夫。福建福州地区流传着这样一句俗语："拔好菜，嫁好婿"。元宵之夜，姑娘们以看灯为借口，偷偷跑到别人家的地里偷菜，偷的数量不多，其偷的目的是为了占卜自己命运。"天青青，月明明，嫦娥引路带我去偷青。偷得洋葱人聪明，偷得生菜招财灵。"每年元宵节，广东封开县封川地区的女性都要到田野里偷生菜和洋葱，相传该习俗起源于纪念孟姜女。孟姜女赶去京城的路途中，饥饿难忍，元宵

晚上忍不住在田野摘了一些蔬菜煮来吃。后来，妇女们为了纪念孟姜女的忠贞，同情她的遭遇，每逢元宵节都举行"偷青"民俗活动。当地妇女相信，元宵节"偷青"意头好，小女孩偷到大葱寓意越来越聪明，未婚女性偷青可望嫁如意郎君，已婚妇女偷到生菜有早生贵子的好兆头。

Chapter Three
The Customs of the Lantern Festival

China has a vast territory with many ethnic groups. Each place has its unique culture and customs. Just take the Lantern Festival as an example, some customs have been commonly observed by Chinese people since the Han Dynasty, such as the lantern show, eating *yuanxiao*, the lantern riddles, and the firework display; some other customs have been only popular in a certain area, like walking for health, welcoming the Purple Goddess, playing dragon lantern, and stealing vegetables.

1. Lantern Show

Lanterns in ancient China were not only a tool for illumination, but a work of art for the Lantern Festival celebration as well. Chinese people have been creating new patterns of lantern constantly, thus the lanterns are in different colors and forms. Since the 15th night of the first lunar month was officially recognized as a national festival in the Han Dynasty, the festival has always been closely connected with lanterns, and many customs related to lanterns have been formed, such as raising lanterns, the lantern show, lantern riddles, lantern couplets and the dragon lantern dance. Considering the importance of lantern show in the whole celebration, people in some places give the festival another name "Lantern Festival".

1.1 Lighting up Lanterns on the 15th Night of the First Lunar Month

Long before, there were many cruel beasts of prey in the

Admiring the Lantern

world, and many people and domestic animals were often hurt or eaten. So people had to think out ways to kill those beasts. One day, a fairy bird in the heaven made a mistake and was degraded to the human world as a punishment, but unfortunately it was shot dead by a hunter who did not know its real identity.

The time of punishment was due but the heaven didn't see the bird back. Hearing of the fairy bird's incident from the king of hell, the Heavenly Emperor flew into a rage and ordered heavenly troops to burn down the human world on the 15th day of the first lunar month.

The Heavenly Emperor had a beautiful and kindhearted daughter who overheard her father's plan. She felt unbearable to see all the common people suffer such a big disaster, so she immediately came to the human world and told people the whole story. But people were doubtful about it until the hunter stood out and confessed his fault for shooting a fairy bird. People began to panic and seek the way out.

A wise old man offered an idea, "In the three days from the 15th day, we could light up lanterns, set off firecrackers and fireworks, which may make the Heavenly Emperor believe that the human world has already been in a big fire." People all thought highly of his suggestion and began to prepare lanterns, firecrackers and fireworks as he said. From the 15th to the 17th night, when the Heavenly Emperor saw the human world in a red halo and endless noises, he felt much relieved. People finally saved themselves. To commemorate the success, every year on this day, all the families would raise lanterns and set off fireworks.

1.2 Huang Chao Raised Lanterns to Protect Common

People

Huang Chao (820 AD—884 AD) was a salt businessman in Caozhou City of the Tang Dynasty. He accumulated a great wealth from business and took in many homeless people. In the late Tang, especially in the reign of Emperor Yizong (860 AD—874 AD), due to the excessive tax and years of floods and droughts, people lived on the edge of starvation. In the meantime, the royal members still enjoyed their extravagant life, and the burglaries and robberies occurred frequently.

Huang Chao was one of those who rose up to resist the imperial court. His soldiers fought hard for three days and still couldn't conquer the capital. Considering it was near the end of the year, he ordered to withdraw. As soon as the Spring Festival was over, Huang alone sneaked into the capital city for military information but he was tracked down by the court. At the very crucial moment, an old man saved him out of trouble and shared his stratagem to strike the court. Huang felt very grateful to the old man and said, "I will come back with my army on the 15th night of the month. I am sure I will conquer the city. Please tell those common people to raise a lantern at their own gates. My army will never enter the houses with lanterns. As for those without lanterns, their owners must be those corrupted officials, and we will not let them live."

On the 15th night, Huang's army successfully conquered the imperial city, and those officials who used to bully people were all killed. To commemorate Huang's righteousness, people observed the custom of raising lanterns on the 15th night of the first lunar month.

2. Lantern Fair

With the popularity of lantern display, the lantern fair was taking its form in many places in China, especially in big cities.

2.1 The History of the Lantern Fair

The Lantern fair in the Tang Dynasty was grander than ever. The Ming Dynasty lengthened the festival and the fair becomes much lively. River lanterns appeared in the Ming Dynasty. When the night fell, people rode a boat to the middle of a river, and then they put lanterns onto the river. The lanterns floated on the water and became a spectacular sight at night. After 1403 AD when Emperor Chengzu moved the capital to Beijing, the Lantern Festival became a holiday for all officials, and a special lantern fair was set up at Donghua Gate for the festival celebration.

In the Qing Dynasty, the lantern fairs in different places had acquired their unique features. In regions south of the Yangtze River, the lantern fair began from the 13th night and ended at the 18th night. As described in documents about Qing Dynasty, "on the 13th night, lanterns in kitchens will be lit and raised until the 18th night." People usually made rice balls (or sweet dumplings) for the dinner on the 13th night, and noodles on the 18th night. In Hangzhou, the dragon lantern had to be taken to Dragon King Temple on the 12th day before it was shown in the fair. In Sichuan, lantern hill was very popular. In the west Sichuan, the lantern fair began on the 9th day of the first lunar month. People in the same neighborhood would take turns to hold parties for gathering. The dinner on the 9th night was called "Trial Lantern Banquet", and the gathering dinners would last until the 16th night. During the dinners, lanterns were raised up in all rooms of each family as a symbol to drive away evil spirits.

2.2 The customs of Festival Lanterns

In ancient China, people lighted up lanterns just to drive away the darkness, and lanterns became a symbol for brightness. However, lanterns on the Lantern Festival have gained more symbolic meanings with the progress of history.

First, lanterns are used to drive away evil spirits. In the Qing Dynasty, a ritual of "illuminating the Evil" was held in Anhui and Hubei provinces with an intention to drive away the evil spirits. In the north of Jiangsu province, people would set a fire in the farming fields on the Lantern Festival, which would burn up the injurious pests and insect eggs and were believed helpful for a good harvest next year. In Shaanxi, local people would light up many lanterns in their houses, and even carried a lantern to illuminate every dark corner inside and outside around their houses. The custom was named "illuminating the dark corners" meaning that the evil had been driven away.

Second, lanterns are good wishes for peace. In Buddhist temples, a "Brightness Lantern" is usually hung up to bless a peaceful year. In rural fields, a lantern is put onto the top of a long bamboo pole, and farmers may predict whether there is a drought or flood next year according to the flame of the lantern. Another custom "flying heavenly lanterns" was said originated from a bandits attack in the past. People under the attack escaped away to different directions and flew the heavenly lanterns as a message of safety to their families. When people went back home, it was just on the 15th day of the first lunar month. Since then, people celebrated the day with flying lanterns, and the lanterns are also called "Praying Lanterns" or "Peace Lanterns". Gradually, flying lanterns became a folk custom to pray for blessings from the heaven. The lanterns contain people's written prayers to the heaven and bring people infinite hopes and brightness.

In the Qing Dynasty, the lanterns were also a carrier of prayers for pregnancy. In the east Sichuan province, people might "steal" lanterns under the eaves. The "stealers" were usually women who had not given birth to a baby, or a boy in most cases. On the Lantern Festival, all the households would raised lanterns under the eaves, "stealers" would sneak into a house whose owner had several children already, and stole one eave lantern as a good omen for their own pregnancy. In Southern Fujian Dialect, lantern sounds like "Ding", meaning "family member", thus the lanterns are used to symbolize a prayer for new birth.

It was said that Emperor Taizong of the Tang Dynasty encouraged schooling. On the first day of school term, every student customarily carried a festival lantern to school, and asked the learned and senior teacher to light it up, which meant "to light up the bright future". The old style private school in China usually began a new schooling term after the Lantern Festival. So the custom was believed to be a follow-up of the festival.

Besides all the above symbolic meanings, what matters most for the festival lanterns is that they should be eye-comforter. Different types and colors made the audience have no time to take in the scene as a whole. The nightscape in the lantern fairs has brought a lot of fun to the people.

2.3 Types of Festival Lanterns

Chinese people have created various festival lanterns with beautiful patterns and brilliant handicraft skills. Among the various festival lanterns with Chinese characteristics, the most famous ones are as follows.

The first is Palace Lantern. Palace lanterns were mainly used in the imperial palace or official residences. And the level of handicraft often symbolized the wealth and luxury of those dignitaries. So palace lanterns were believed to be the most distinguished in Chinese lanterns. The unearthed oldest palace lantern is the Changxin Palace Lantern of the Western Han Dynasty. The lantern is shaped into a figure of a maid on her knees holding a copper lantern. The lantern has not many decorations and complicated patterns on the surface. In Beijing's Palace Museum, the oldest palace lanterns in store are the ones of the Ming Dynasty.

Beijing Palace Lantern has enjoyed a long reputation in the field of handicrafts. There is a silk painting lantern with strong palace features, of which the hexagon palace lantern is the most typical one. It has double layers in space, with 6 short pillars on the upper level with carved dragon and phoenix and 6 longer pillars on the lower level with hallowed petals. Silk paintings are set between those pillars which featured auspicious and legendary animals and birds. In 1915, Beijing Palace Lanterns were put on display in the Panama Pacific International Exposition and won the gold award. Based on the traditional hexagon lanterns, the modern people have designed the new festival lanterns with elegant carving skills using the precious wood such as rosewood and sandalwood. The types are developed to hanging lanterns, wall lanterns, table lanterns and standing lanterns. Beijing Palace Lantern is a multi-crafted artwork involving over 100 procedures like carpentry, carving, lacquering, knitting and painting. Some complex lanterns may even take months to finish.

Tuntou village in Gaocheng, Hebei province is known as the town of palace lanterns. In the Ming Dynasty, a craftsman in this village was a master in making silk lanterns, and his lanterns were exquisite and durable, thus were very popular with governmental organizations and rich families. In the Qing Dynasty, Emperor Qianlong liked such lanterns very much when he visited the south of China, and took some lanterns back to the imperial palace. As for why the Gaocheng Lantern became the palace lantern, there is another story. In the reign of Emperor Yongzheng of Qing Dynasty, an old man in Tuntou village was very good at making lanterns. Every year on the Spring Festival, he would hang up pairs of shining lanterns at the gate of his house which attracted many people to observe. Even the magistrate of Gaocheng was fond of those lanterns very much and bought them all in. The time to pay tribute to the emperor had come, but the magistrate could not think out any other presents but the lanterns. Feeling a little reluctance, he sent those lanterns to the palace. To his surprise, Emperor Yongzheng liked those lanterns too, rewarded him heavily, and granted this kind of lanterns as the regular tributes. Since then, the bright red lanterns appeared on each corner of imperial palaces and gradually became the exclusive "Tribute Lanterns" for the palace. And that was the origin of palace lanterns today.

The second is Suzhou Lantern. As early as in the Song Dynasty, Suzhou Lanterns had already formed an independent trade of handicrafts. The lanterns have a beautiful design, bright color and delicate appearance with integration of painting, paper-cutting, paper-pasting, paper-strapping, knitting, embroidery, carving, clay figurine, and silk figurine. Different from other lanterns, Suzhou Lanterns combine architecture art of classical Suzhou gardens and Wu-style painting in the Ming Dynasty. The main frame features airy pavilions and pagodas, and the inside decorations are color paintings of figures, mountains, water, flowers, birds or animals with South China characteristics. Running Horse Lantern is the most ingenious one. Its main structure is a green-tiled pavilion, and there are two layers of indistinct patterns on the inside wall which can revolve by air current convection after the candle is lit up. Thus the revolving patterns look like a living picture to the observers.

The third is Xiashi Lantern. As early as in the Song Dynasty, Xiashi Lanterns in Haining City, Zhejiang Province, were chosen as the tribute to the imperial palace. This kind of lantern specialized in needling work, with thin bamboo strip as the frame. The paintings and patterns on the paper are entirely manual needling work.

Besides, the famous festival lanterns include Lotus Lanterns in Nanjing Confucius Temple, Track Lanterns in Huangyuan of Qinghai, Quanzhou Flower Lanterns, Wenzhou Pearl Lanterns, and Shanghai Goldfish Wall Lanterns. All are marvelous. In some places, people even make flour lanterns. First, shape dough into different designs such as a bowl, a bell, a wine-cup, or a bottle; then steam them; after cooling them down, add soya-bean oil and wick into the steamed dough, then the flour lantern is ready for use. To make the Flour Lantern colorful, people just use different kinds of flour: the corn flour for Golden Lantern, wheat flour for Silvery Lantern, buckwheat flour for Iron Lantern. Some even make use of colored paper to paste a lantern, or glass slices to assemble a lantern decorated with colored paper-cuts; those lanterns look gorgeous under the candle light.

In modern times, people can enjoy not only the traditional festival lanterns, but also some hi-tech products like acoustic-controlled ones, light-operated ones, magnetic controlled ones, or remote controlled ones. When observers clap their hands, the acoustic-controlled lanterns will shine sparklingly.

Tips for Tourism

the Nanjing Confucius Temple

The Nanjing Confucius Temple is located at Gongyuan Street, on the north bank of Qinhuai River and to the west of the Jiangnan Imperial Examination Center. As one of the four great temples of the Sage of Literature in China, it is built to worship and offer sacrifices to Confucius. It is not only Nanjing's education center in Ming and Qing Dynasties, but also the symbolic cultural architectural complex in the southeast of China. Now, it has become an important part of Qinhuai Scenic Zone.

Covering a huge area, the Nanjing Confucius Temple is mainly composed of three grand ancient buildings, the temples, the schools, and the examination halls. The famous scenic spots include Screen Wall, School Front Pool, Archway, Juxing Pavilion, Kuixing Tower, Lingxing Gate, Dacheng Hall, Mingde Hall, and Zunjing Hall. It is the biggest traditional street in China, and one of the four busiest streets in modern China.

Routes:

1. Take the airport shuttle bus at Lukou station and get off at Zhonghua Gate, then take subway L1 to Sanshanjie station, about 1 hour; or take airport line to Nanjing South Railway Station, then take subway L1 to Sanshanjie station, about 1 hour.

2. Take bus at Nanjing Railway Station and get off at Confucius Temple station, or take subway L1 at the railway station to Sanshanjie station, and exit from the L3 gate and walk straight to the east until you'll get to the Confucius Temple.

3. Eating *Yuanxiao*

Yuanxiao, a sweet ball dumpling, is a traditional food in China that cannot be neglected on the Lantern Festival. The night of the Lantern Festival is also a full-moon night symbolizing the family reunion, and that is why the *yuanxiao* is made in the circular form. In Chinese culture, circular form means harmony, tolerance, perfection, and reunion as well.

The custom of eating *yuanxiao* originated from the Song Dynasty. And at that time it was named *tangyuan*, pastry, sweet balls, soup balls, water balls... Those different names tell us clearly the big variety of *yuanxiao* in the Song Dynasty. *The Old Story of Wulin* by Zhou Mi also recorded, "The festival food includes no other kind but milk sugar balls, tadpole-shaped snack, and salted bean soup." The making of *Yuanxiao* has become more delicate since the Ming Dynasty. Liu Ruoyu

Sweet ball Dumplings

in the Ming Dynasty recorded the recipe of *Yuanxiao* in *ZhuoZhongzhi*(Notes on Events and Proceedings in the Ming Dynasty), "Knead the glutinous rice flour to shape the dough. Pinch off a piece of dough approximately the size of a golf ball. Roll the dough into a ball. Place a walnut seed and white sugar into a ball. Cook the ball dumplings in boiled water and then the *Yuanxiao* (or *tangyuan* in the south) are available for dinner." The method was quite similar to today's.

Eating *Yuanxiao* on the Lantern Festival has already become a traditional custom for Chinese people. If one has not eaten *Yuanxiao* on the 15th day of the first lunar month, he or she is believed not to have departed the old year completely. Eating *Yuanxiao* becomes a symbol for family reunion.

As a festival food, *Yuanxiao* contains many cultural elements. Different places have developed different methods in making *Yuanxiao*, and diversified regional cuisine cultures.

Generally speaking, *Yuanxiao* mainly uses glutinous rice flour, sorghum flour, millet flour, corn flour or purple rice flour as the raw materials. There are solid balls and filling balls. The fillings can be sweet or salt according to one's taste. The sweet fillings can be made of either of the following ingredients: sweetened bean paste in lard oil, white sugar sesame, osmanthus mixture, jujube paste, nuts, sesame paste, almond, ginkgo, and hawthorn berry. The salted fillings are made of either fresh diced meat, or ham or small shrimp. People may also choose vegetable fillings which are composed of mustard, onion, garlic, chives, and ginger. This is named Five Flavors *Yuanxiao* which symbolizes the spirit of industry, longevity, and progress. However, the cooking of *Yuanxiao* can be diversified, either water-boiled, or stir fried, deep-fired or steamed. When boiling the *Yuanxiao*, one may add fermented glutinous rice, white sugar and fragrans, thus the final delicious soup is mixed with the flavors of glutinous rice, fillings, and other seasonings. The practices may diverse from place to place. In the north of China, people usually roll the sweet balls with a bamboo basket, while in the south, people use hand-rolling. *Yuanxiao* can be as big as walnuts, or as small as soya beans.

Why do Chinese people eat *yuanxiao* for the festival? There are some folk stories.

3.1 King Zhao of Chu State and *Yuanxiao*

One day in the late Spring and Autumn Period, King Zhao (523 BC—489 BC) of Chu State came across a white ball-shape stuff floating on the river on his way home. He ordered boatmen to drag for it. After cutting the ball stuff open, he found this kind of fruit had rouge-red fruit meat and appealing fragrance. He tasted it and was greatly pleased at its sweetness. But nobody around knew the fruit. King Zhao sent for an answer from Confucius. Confucius said that the fruit was named Rising Fruit, and it was a good sign for the reviving of the kingdom. King Zhao got greatly rejoiced. Since it was just on the Lantern Festival, he ordered people to model the fruit and cook flour balls, or *yuanxiao*, for good luck. Since then, *yuanxiao* became a necessary food for the Lantern Festival.

3.2 Chang'e and *Tangyuan*

There is a story in the Yuan Dynasty. After Chang'e flew to the moon, her husband Houyi missed her very much and fell ill. On the 14th night of the first lunar month, a boy messenger was sent by Chang'e to tell Houyi that Chang'e was also missing him very much but she had already become an immortal and could not fly back to the earth. However, the boy also told Houyi a way to see Chang'e. He asked Houyi to make moon-like balls with rice flour on the 15th full-moon night, and put them at the northwest of the house, then call out Chang'e's name continuously, and then Chang'e could fly back to the earth only at the midnight. Houyi did everything the boy told him to do and anxiously waited for Chang'e. At the midnight, Chang'e flew back as expected. The couple finally could meet each other and express their affections. Since then, *tangyuan* has been regarded as a food for reunion blessing. On every Lantern Festival, people will definitely eat *tangyuan* with a hope of family reunion and happy life.

3.3 Yuan Shikai and *Yuanxiao*

After the Revolution of 1911, Yuan Shikai (1859 AD— 1916 AD) became the first president after North-South Peace Talks during the revolution. However, after he usurped the fruits of the revolution, he wanted to maintain the monarchy, but he was also afraid of people's opposition and lived in a anxious life. One day, he heard some people hawking "*yuanxiao*" loudly in the streets which sounded identical to "remove Yuan". Yuan felt very upset. Before the Lantern Festival in 1913, he banned the name of *yuanxiao*, and only allowed people to use "tangyaun" or "fenguo". However, the name "*yuanxiao*" has not vanished as he wished; the common people didn't show respect for his order and still used the name of "*yuanxiao*".

4. Lantern Riddles

Riddles first appeared in the Spring and Autumn Period (770 BC—476 BC), and they were called "hidden language" at that time. It was only until the Song Dynasty that riddles became a part of the Lantern Festival celebration. In some places, it was called "to break the lantern riddles". People wrote a riddle on a piece of paper and paste it onto a lantern for other people to guess the meaning. As for why it has become a part of festival celebration, a folk story says so:

Long ago, there was a rich man Hu who always showed a foxy smile to others but ran wild in the village, thus villagers called him "Smiling Tiger". Hu often judged people by their outer appearances. For those well dressed, he just curried favour with them; for those in rags, he looked like a devil with eyebrows pointing to the sky.

One day before the Spring Festival, two men came to the door of Hu. One was named Li Cai who was in a decent and colored clothes. The other was Wang Shao in ragged clothes. However, when Hu's servant saw Li Cai and immediately went to report. Smiling Tiger hurriedly came out and gave Li a warm reception. Li asked confidently, "Please lend me some money." Smiling Tiger did not hesitate to deliver the money to him. Li

Guessing Lantern Riddles

went away with great satisfaction.

Just then, Wang Shao went forward and said, "Master, I have no more food at home. Could you lend me some grain?" Smiling Tiger turned round and gave Wang a glimpse. Seeing him in a worn-out clothes, Smiling Tiger stamped with rage, "You poor chap, leave me alone." Wang was driven away by Hu's servants, having no time to argue.

On the way home, Wang felt angrier at it. Suddenly a good idea occurred to him, and he was determined to get even with the Smiling Tiger. Soon the Spring Festival was over and the Lantern Festival came. Colorful lanterns were hung at the gates of each house, and Wang also carried a lantern to the street. His lantern was made in a whole day, bright and big, unique enough, with a poem written on it.

Wang came to the door of Hu, and raised the lantern high to attract the audience. Smiling Tiger was just at the gate and moved forward to observe the lantern. However, Hu didn't know all the characters on the lantern, thus he asked his accountant to read for him. The accountant read the poem word by word, "pointed head, slender body, as white as silver, light-weight. The eyes are strangely on the butt, and only recognize clothes but not people."

The Smiling Tiger heard it and got red in his face. He shouted, "How dare you! How could you abuse me?" He then asked his servants to rob him of the lantern. Wang hurriedly raised the lantern up and smiled, "Master, how did you know I was abusing you?" Hu shouted, "Look at your poem! Isn't it abusing me that I only recognize clothes not people?" Wang read the poem again and laughed, "No. No. No. Master, you are mistaking it and scolding yourself. My poem is a riddle, and the answer is 'Needle'. Don't you think so?" The Smiling Tiger finally realized the key to the riddle, and felt angrily ashamed. He could not say any words but go away in embarrassment. All the people around laughed heartily.

The next day, the news of Wang's poking fun at Hu with a lantern riddle was spread to the far. After that, people began to prepare riddles on the Festival Lanterns. If any observers guessed the riddles correctly, they might get a reward, and that was called "Shooting Tiger Lanterns." Gradually it became a custom for the Lantern Festival which is still popular in many places up to now.

Lantern riddle is a very witty game which takes full use of the polysemy of Chinese characters and the answers of the riddles are normally not the literal meaning of riddles. Now, lantern riddles have added fun and joy to the Lantern Festival, and also have brought about happiness and peace.

5. Lantern Couplets

Couplet, also called distich, is one of the cultural treasures in China. Couplets are antithetical pair of lines in rhyme and have the same meter in poetry written on paper, cloth, or carved on bamboo, wood. A complete couplet consists of two lines, and the festival couplets often are added with another horizontal scroll bearing an inscription.

Lantern couplets are pasted on festival lanterns or in a lantern fair, usually with two lines. Since festival couplets could add great joy to the celebration, people began to paste lantern couplets at the gate and obvious pillars. Some men of letters might produce the first line of a lantern couplet and waited other lantern observers to supply the second line. In ancient

China, on the Lantern Festivals, it was a wonderful choice to drink together, enjoy lanterns and discuss about the lantern couplets. Lantern couplets have become an important custom for the Lantern Festival.

There are many interesting folk stories about lantern couplets. One of them is about Wang Anshi (1021 AD—1086 AD), a famous statesman in the Northern Song Dynasty. Wang went to Beijing for the imperial exam when he was 20 and arrived in a beautiful city on the Lantern Festival. He was attracted by the beautiful scenery and stopped to observe the lanterns there. When he passed by a house of a rich family, he found a pair of couplets on a running horse lantern. The family wanted to select a bridegroom for their daughter from those who could complete the couplets. The first line of couplets said, "The horse is running in the rotating lantern, and it stops when the lantern is extinguished." Wang could not give an answer but just memorized it in heart. When he arrived in Beijing he found it was coincidental that the exam question was just to complete the following couplet "The tiger is flying on the flaunting flag, and it hides inside

Guessing Lantem Riddles

when the flag is rolled up." Wang answered with the former couplet and became a successful candidate. When he went back to the rich family and found still nobody had answered the couplets. He soon completed the couplets by the exam question, and was finally selected as the bridegroom.

In the Qing Dynasty, there were a father and a son who both became a scholar and prime minister. The father was Zhang Ying, and the son was Zhang Tingyu. One year's Lantern Festival, the Zhang residence was decorated with all kinds of festival lanterns and firecrackers were set off. The senior Zhang offered a couplet "Burn the red candle in high place and brightness is spread all over the ground." The junior Zhang heard a loud bang of firecracker and immediately replied, "Light the festival sparkler at low ground, and sound is roaring towards the sky." The pair of couplets is full of ingenuity with careful and perfect antithesis.

Another prodigy in the Qing Dynasty was Min Eyuan in Wuxing of Zhejiang Province. He was known for finishing couplets at a fast speed. On a Lantern Festival, he followed his father to attend a friend's home party. It was just a dim night when clouds covered the moon. Another guest offered a couplet for the occasion, "There is no moon on the Lantern Festival, so let's light up lanterns to brighten the earth." All the guests fell in deep thinking. After a while, still no one answered. Min Eyuan just then heard a drum beat from afar and put up an answer, "There is no thunder on the Waking of Insects, so let's beat drums to dignify the sky." All the people were amazed at his perfect completion of the couplets.

6. Lantern Poetry

Men of letters in the past centuries have created lots of poems about the Lantern Festival and many are passed down to today. To review the past scenery described in the poems, modern people write those poems on the festival lanterns. Those lantern poems cover all aspects of the festival, and some are describing the scenery of the day, such as Tang poet Guo Lizhen's *Upper Yuan Festival*:

"Nine streets in the brightness of lanterns, thousands of houses in the moonlight. Horse carriages and elegant sedans come and go endlessly. Intoxicated in the night scenery, people even forget to come back home. When the crackers set off in the sky, plum blossoms fall to the ground."

Some other poems are expressing the personal feelings on the festival, just like Northern Song poet Qin Guan wrote in his poem *Love of Butterfly*:

"This year's Lantern Festival, the moon is so bright and full that I couldn't help missing the mountains at my hometown. How I want to ride a horse! The road is so long that my dream even can't fly over. Only I could walk lonely in the bright moonlight."

The writer was far away from home, and the solitude and loneliness made him homesick and began to imagine the festival excitement in his hometown.

7. Dragon Lanterns

Dragon is an auspicious legendary animal in Chinese culture. Dragon lanterns, also called dragon lantern dancing, or dragon dance, dated back to the ancient times. It is said that as early as in the times of the Yellow Emperor, the image of dragon-head and bird-body had already been created in a large scale dance. And later, the image of six dragons intertwined with each other also appeared in dancing. The earliest written record about dragon dance is *Western Metropolis Rhapsody* by Zhang Heng in the Han Dynasty, which gives vivid description of dragon dance.

In the minds of ancient Chinese people, dragon is a supernatural animal that controls wind and rain, and removes ill fortune. On important festivals and occasions, worshiping dragon is believed to pray for a favorable weather and good harvest, and the dragon dance is also for the same reason. Wu Zimu of the Song Dynasty recorded in *Menglianglu*, "On the Lantern Festival, people weave a dragon with grass, and cover it with green cloth. Thousands of candles are placed inside the dragon body. Looking from afar, it seems that two wriggling dragons are flying over the field." From the records, it can be known that the dragon at that time was made of grass, and of

Dragon Lantern Dance

109

course the materials became diversified afterwards. The dragon lantern is usually made of thin bamboo strips. In the front is the dragon head, and the body is composed of unfixed sections in odd numbers, each section supported by a stick. Candles are set in each section. The dragon dances usually theme on two types: one dragon plays with a pearl, and two dragons grabs a pearl. When performing the dance, one man holds a colorful "pearl" to lure "dragons". The person with the dragon head runs after the pearl, and consequently, other performers holding their consecutive sections follow to move up and down, left and right, with the accompaniment of gongs and drums. The sight is really magnificent.

8. Fireworks Display

In many important festival celebrations, a fireworks display is a necessary ceremony. On the New Year's Eve, a fireworks

Setting off Fireworks

110

display means to ring out the old year and ring in the new year. And on the night of Lantern Festival, it means the end of the Spring Festival celebration.

Fireworks have a long history in China, so the technology and variety are much developed into a high level. The most famous is Flower Box which unfolds a clear picture of figures, birds and flowers in the mist of fireworks under the moon-lit night. In the late Qing Dynasty, a kind of Flower Box, named Fireworks City, was exclusively made for the imperial palace. The Fireworks City was a mini-city structure, with towers over four gates, bridges, flags, and guards. When it was lit up, all the "lanterns" on the city walls showed off brightness, then the bridge slumped and many lotus flowers appeared on the bridge. Another firework was named Beauty in Pavilion. When it was lit up, it looked like a beauty dancing in the pavilion in the light of bead lanterns under the roof. Flower Archway was a line of animal images under a big archway, lion, elephant, tiger and leopard with Chinese characters " 万 寿 无 疆 " on their foreheads. When it was fired, fireworks flew 1 or 2 meters high from the bottles on the back of the elephant. The other animals either vomited blazes, or shoot cylindrical fireworks, all their eyes emitting lotus flames. When it was burned down, all animals kneed down and prayed for longevity.

Now in China, some local governments may choose a particular place for fireworks displays. Since each firework needs several minutes to burn down, it takes a relatively long time to watch the entire display. Some common people may purchase fireworks by themselves, normally small-sized ones for family celebration.

9. Stilts Walking

Walking on Stilts is a very popular mass performance in the Lantern Festival celebration. It has other names like High Stilts, Stilt Steps, Strapping Stilts, or Walking Stilts. It is said that the ancient people bound two stilts to their legs for the ease of collecting fruits from trees, and later it was developed into a skilled activity. In the past people dug out a pedal in the middle of a wood stick, and then bound the stick to one's leg with ropes. Walking on Stilts, one of the variety shows in ancient China, came into existence in the Spring and Autumn Period.

As for the origin of Walking on Stilts, there are different versions. It was said that in the Spring and Autumn Period, a man named Yan Ying had worked as a minister for three kings in Qi Kingdom. Once, Yan was sneered at by some ministers of a neighboring country during a diplomatic visit, just because he was too short in height. He was so angry that he tied his legs to a pair of wood sticks, which made all the ministers feel amused. He got even offended, and began to mimic those ministers until they were embarrassed. Gradually, Walking on Stilts spread to the common people as a form of amusement.

Another story says that the Walking on Stilts has something to do with corrupt and evil officials. Once in Liangjin County, community fairs for business and harvest were regularly held between people in and out of the county. But the corrupt official of this place took the fair as an opportunity to make money, and ordered all men participating in the fair to pay extra 11 grams of silver. People were all resentful towards it and nobody followed the rule. The official then shut the gate of the county and hung up the drawbridge over the fosse river. People outside the county were clever enough and produced long walking stilts with which they could cross the walls and the moat of the county. The official had no choice but to give up his evil idea. Walking on Stilts as a festival custom has remained until now.

The modern stilts are much similar to the ancient ones, and the performers usually wear costumes. There are three kinds of stilts, high stilts, medium-sized stilts and running stilts. The highest one may reach over 3 meters. During the show, performers will do many skilled movements on stilts such as sword-show, splits, stool-leap, table-leap, and yangko dance. Each actor will play a role in Chinese traditional dramas. They dance and sing as if they are standing on the flat ground, and the audience are frequently amused by their extravagant movements.

10. Lion Dance

Lion dance is also named Peace Music. In Chinese history, lions were not aboriginal animals in the Central Plains, but an

Lion Dance

article of tribute brought by Zhang Qian, a diplomat, from the Western Regions in the reign of Emperor Wu of Han Dynasty, and peacocks were also brought into Han at that time. In legend, lions were Manjuist Bodhisattva's beast for riding, and the statue of lion flourished when Buddhism was introduced into China. And lion dance originated from a mask drama in Xiliang (today's Jiuquan and Dunhuang area, in the west of Gansu Province).

Chinese people traditionally believed that lion dance could drive out evil spirits and ghosts, so on every Lantern Festival or celebration, lion dance is an indispensable item. Many people believed that the custom began in the period of Three Kingdoms, and developed in the Northern and Southern Dynasties, but flourished in the Tang Dynasty. Lion dance is usually played by three people, two dressed as a lion (one holding the lion head, and the other acting as the body and the back legs), and the third person as a lion trainer. Lion dance can be categorized into civilian lion and martial lion according to the performing styles. The civilian lion dance emphasizes the agility and docility of lions with movements like trembling and rolling; the martial lion dance shows the ferocity and power of the lion in galloping, falling and tumbling. Now in China, lion dance is popular in many places on the Lantern Festival.

11. The Swing

In ancient times, the primitive tribes in the north of China created the swing when climbing trees to get food at a high place. It was called "Qian Qiu" at the beginning. The first swing was just a long rope that people could hold around. Later in the Spring and Autumn Period, the swing was introduced into the Central Plains by Duke Huan of Qi when conquering the north tribes. In the reign of Emperor Wu in the Han Dynasty, "Qian Qiu" became a popular greeting for birthday congratulations, meaning longevity, which was later changed into "Qiu Qian" for taboo consideration. Then the swing activity was developed into a tread plate hung on a frame by two long ropes. It soon became popular among common people by its easy access and simple rules. Since the Han Dynasty, the swing has already become a folk sport on the Lantern Festival and the Dragon Boat Festival until today.

Now on every Lantern Festival, the swing activity is very popular in some places such as Wu'an City, She County, and Ci County in Hebei Province. From the 10th day of the first lunar month, the local people put up swing brackets of different heights at an open area in the village or in their own yards. The villagers play it every day until the 16th day, and the climax appears on the 14th and 15th day. People believe that the swing could dispel diseases and sicknesses which may well explain why it can be spread from generation to generation over different dynasties. The kids and the old are willing to try it even with other people's help. Swinging can be categorized into the single swing, double swing, standing swing and sitting swing. Each village in Hebei has some top players and sometimes competitions are held for them. The ones who swing the highest or the most difficult will be a "big star" in the neighborhood. For young men and women, swinging is also a good opportunity to be acquainted with each other.

12. Mouse Chasing

In Wei and Jin Dynasties, a new custom for the Lantern

Festival celebration appeared in the southern areas with bountiful silkworm production. During the days of the Lantern Festival, mice began to run around the farmland slowly and sluggishly. It was the best time to kill the destructive animals. However in the past, the mouse was regarded as a god of five cereals and could not be killed easily, so people had to play up to it in belief that the mouse could leave away from their silkworm. On the Lantern Festival, a pot of meat gruel was placed at a spot the mouse often passed by; a curse was made at the same time that if the mouse still brought trouble after it ate the gruel, the mouse would face death.

Another story proves the fact that the people used gruel to pray for silkworm harvest. Long long ago in Wu County, a man named Zhang Cheng woke up at a midnight and saw a beautiful girl standing at the southeast corner of his yard. The girl waved to him and he stepped forward. Then the girl said, "I am the god of this place. On the next Lantern Festival, if you offer gruel and meat to me as a sacrifice, your silkworm will have a good harvest." Then she disappeared. Zhang did everything as the fairy said, and it turned out to be true that he had a good harvest in the silkworm. So he did the same since then and had a bumper harvest year by year.

In some other places, people had other similar customs to drive away mice. In Ningxiang County of Hunan Province, people dip the incense into tea oil and burn it at every corner of their houses to protect grains and belongings from mice; some people even read incantations to drive mice away.

13. Lantern Gifts

On the Lantern Festival, people usually send lanterns to

their daughters as gifts, and to gods as sacrifice.

In Chinese language, lantern pronounces similar to "ding", which means new born babies. In some areas, parents, relatives and friends may send lanterns to a newly-wed as a best wish for giving birth to a baby. On the first year of the new marriage, the bride's parents might give festival lanterns, usually a pair of palace lanterns, to the new couple during the Lantern Festival. If their daughter has already been pregnant at that moment, they need to give two extra pairs of smaller lanterns with candles lit until the night. Such gifted lanterns are called Baby Lanterns symbolizing good wishes for peaceful pregnancy. The tradition varies in different places but it mainly focuses on praying for new babies.

On the festival day, some villages may hold lantern sacrifices to gods. The villagers will parade through the village, holding a festival lantern, beating drums and gongs, and setting up firecrackers, and finally they put up the lantern in the

Lantern Gifts in Wenchang, Hainan

117

temple of the village. When the lantern is ready, all the villagers will go further to jostle for the lanterns since they believe that whoever get the lantern will make a good fortune and add new family members next year. In some other areas, people will prepare lots of lanterns and light them up before the sunset. They will first send lanterns to the front of their ancestor's spirit tablet for a blessing of family peace and prosperity. Then they send the lanterns to the tablets of gods for happiness. Later they send them to such places as warehouse, animal pens, wells, and grinding room, in the hope of good harvest, healthy animals, and peaceful life. Further to the crossroad to pray for peaceful transportation and frequent receptions. In the end, the eldest son of each family will send basketful flour lanterns and other lanterns to the ancestral graves. On the way they keep silence as a respect for ancestors in the front of graves, they could not borrow a match but use their own to light up the lanterns; if not, it means they could not pass the days by themselves. The candles in the lanterns should be red or yellow green in color and the white candle in front of the graves is forbidden, because it is believed the white candle means a single and blank life of a bachelor. After placing the lanterns well in front of the grave, they have to scatter the mixture of oil and grain bran in the shape of square around the grave, only leaving a hole at the southwest corner as a gate where an iron lantern is placed. Then they light up the grain bran, and a fire dragon is formed with the help of wind. The Fire Dragon is said to bring good fortune to the ancestor's grave. Finally the iron lantern is lit up to show the way to heaven for the spirits. Those people kowtow and pray for a while before they go home.

In Wenchang City, Hainan Province, it is a tradition to

send lanterns as gifts. On the 15th night of the first lunar month, people take along festival lanterns on each of which printed 72 big or small characters of "happiness" and 36 characters of "longevity", on the front are auspicious words like "amassing wealth" or "more babies" or some figure and landscape paintings. The lantern parade, led by a "lantern leader", goes around the village to the temple nearby with the company of drums, gongs and firecrackers. When the lanterns are hung up inside and around the temple, all the village people rush forward to jostle for the lanterns, as those lanterns are believed to bring fortune and babies to the owners. Selecting the lantern leaders also needs special attention. In local dialect, lantern pronounces similar to new born babies,which means "ding". So the lantern leader is acted in turn by those who has a boy at home, and they are mainly in charge of fund collection, coordination of performance, dance, sacrifice, gifted lanterns and other matters. All the people in the parade are from the households with a boy. At the same time there are also some other entertainment activities like Cup-Tray Dance, puppet drama, and Hainan drama.

14. Purple Goddess

There are many legends about the origin of Purple Goddess in China. One has it that before she became the Purple Goddess she was a small concubine in a big family. She could not bear maltreatment and torture from other concubines thus she committed suicide on the 15th day of the first lunar month. Another legend comes from *Romance of the Investiture of the Gods*. Three fairies named Yunxiao, Qiongxiao and Zixiao came to the Yellow River to revenge for their brother

Zhao Gongming (who was later bestowed the Fortune God) who was killed in a war when he helped fight for King Zhou of Shang Dynasty. The three fairies arranged a battle array and trapped the opponents with a magic golden cup. Later when the battle array was damaged by the god of the Original Beginning, the three fairies were also gone with it. Since their weapon—the magic golden cup—was actually a closet tool, they were bestowed as Three Toilet Goddesses. The third version says that the Purple Goddess was named He Mei whose husband was killed by Li Jing, a feudal prefectural governor in Shouyang. Later she was taken in to be a concubine of Li. However her trouble had not ended. On the night of Lantern Festival, she was killed in the toilet by Li's wife out of jealousy. He Mei's spirit did not go away and kept crying in the toilet. The Heavenly Emperor pitied her and bestowed her as the Toilet Goddess.

The purposes to welcome the Purple Goddess are different in places but they are mostly about fortune telling and silkworm. The fortune-telling is usually held near the toilets or pig pens. Some people even wrap up a broom with old clothes, or make a human-shaped figure with grass and corn stalk, and then paste colored paper on it. Then they will paint a face of the Purple Goddess and read incantations, "The husband is absent, and the wife is gone, so the goddess can come out." If the broom becomes heavy, which means the goddess has come and one can ask questions that can be answered with numbers, then the broom is said to be able to nod. In some other places, people carry pigs instead of brooms. If the pig becomes heavy, one can foretell the fortune.

In Jiangsu and Zhejiang Provinces where the silkworm

industry is prosperous, people just welcome the Purple Goddess to foretell the harvest of silkworms.

15. Walking For Health

In the Ming and Qing Dynasties, Walking for Health was a popular folk activity in some places on the 15th day of the first lunar month. On the nights of the Lantern Festival, women all came to the streets to join the walking parade. The parade leader would hold a burning incent in hands, and others followed to travel across every bridge, along every wall and even to the suburb of the town. People believed that it could bring good health and longevity. In some places, women had to not only walk for health, but also touch the round nails on the city gates and temple gates. Because nails in Chinese sounds similar to "ding", meaning boys. So, at that night, women rushed to the city gates and temples to touch the gate nails. Of course, no illuminators were allowed to use in the process, and those who successfully touched the nails would be regarded as having good luck to give birth to a boy. However, in modern times, not only women, but the seniors, the children and people in poor health as well have joined the walking parade.

16. Delightful Stealing

There was another interesting custom of the lantern celebration in the past. It was called "delightful stealing", thus in some places the festival was also named "stealing-and-returning festival." The strange custom began in the Liao Dynasty which allowed people to steal whatever they wanted on the Lantern Festival and without any legal punishment. While in other days, stealing was a serious crime and the

121

punishment would be quite heavy.

The *Brief Account of the Sights of the Imperial Capital* written in 1635 mentioned a three-day stealing customs on the Lantern Festival in the Jin Dynasty. The Khitan people in the Northern and Southern Dynasties had a three-day stealing custom on the 13th, 14th and 15th nights of the first lunar month, while the Nuchen people on the 16th night. The mutual stealing developed greatly into Wei, Qi, and Sui Dynasties and partly in the following dynasties. However, the "stealing" were not really for money, but for good luck. And the one being stolen did not feel sad at all. They stole things of each other just for fun.

According to *The Sketches in Jin Dynasty* by Hong Hao in the Song Dynasty, on the Lantern Festival, some rich women might steal items when they visited other people, and if they were discovered, they just had to offer some tea or cakes as punishment. In different places, the items for stealing were different. Some stole lanterns, some others vegetables. Stealing lanterns and offering lanterns were very popular at that time since it meant a good wish for giving birth to a boy. In the Song Dynasty, it was believed that the lanterns used on the festival night could help women become pregnant. If a couple stole a lantern together and put it under their bed, the woman would soon be pregnant. There was a ballad popular among the people, "If you steal a lantern from Liu's, you may get a baby at the same year. If it is a girl, it is named Dengge (Lantern Guy); if it is a boy, it is named Dengcheng (Lantern Success)." In some places, people would make lanterns with bean flour or carved turnips. Those women who wanted to have a baby would steal those edible lanterns especially from those families whose family name was Liu or Dai, because in Chinese language, Liu sounds similar to "keep a baby", and Dai sounds similar to "bring a baby."

The custom of vegetable stealing still remained in some places of China. In Taiwan, the unmarried women will steal onions or other vegetables on the Lantern Festival in order to have an auspicious blessing to marry a good husband. In Fuzhou of Fujian Province, a common saying has it, "Pluck good vegetables and marry good husband." On the night of the Lantern Festival, girls may tiptoe their way to other people's fields and steal vegetables, not too much but only for a blessing and fortune telling. "Blue sky and bright moon. Chang'e the Fairy leads me to the vegetable field. Stealing an onion makes one wise, and stealing a lettuce brings wealth." In Fengkai County of Guangzhou Province, women steal onions and vegetables on the Lantern Festival and believe that their tradition derives from Meng Jiangnv in the Qin Dynasty. The legend says that on the way to the capital city Meng was so hungry that she could not help plucking some vegetables for food. Later to commemorate her loyalty in love, people hold the folk activity "stealing vegetables" on every Lantern Festival. The local women believe that different age group should steal different things for good omens: little girls should steal an onion for a clever mind; an unmarried woman should steal green vegetables for a good marriage; and a married woman, a lettuce for new birth.

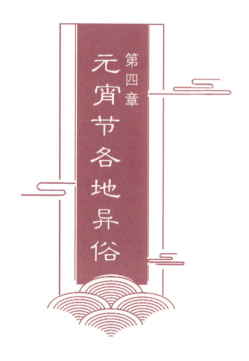

第四章
元宵节各地异俗

中国幅员辽阔，各地的元宵节也有着不同的风俗习惯。江南、东北、西北、台湾等地的元宵节风格迥异，形成了一幅多姿多彩的节庆画卷。

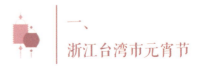

一、
浙江台湾市元宵节

　　与其他地方相比，浙江省台州市的元宵节在起源、节期和饮食方面都有自己独特之处。中国很多地方的元宵节是正月十五，而台州却定在正月十四，之所以比其他地方提前一天，与台州市元宵节的起源相关。

○台州市 2007 年元宵节灯展现场

（一）方国珍的故事

在中国元朝末年有一个农民领袖，他的名字叫方国珍，为台州人。那个时候，在元朝统治者的压迫下，人民无法生活，被迫奋起反抗。方国珍召集各方人士，举行了反抗元朝的起义运动。他占据了温州、台州、宁波三地，并在临海建国称王。后来，反元的各路起义军陷入争权斗争，方国珍担心元军趁元宵佳节前来偷袭，于是就提早一天过元宵节。另外，方国珍很孝敬母亲，因为他母亲信奉佛教，每月初一、十五都要吃素，还要去朝拜寺庙。他为了让母亲也能和家人一起享受节日的快乐，就把元宵节提前了一天。

（二）戚继光抗倭故事

台州正月十四闹元宵还与明朝抗倭名将戚继光有关。传说明朝嘉靖年间（公元1522年—1566年），戚继光在台州一带指挥抗击倭寇时，因为军中的机密被泄露，于是把元宵节提前了一天。作

○戚继光雕像

战胜利后，台州百姓们为了纪念戚继光将军的功绩，就沿袭了正月十四过元宵节的习俗。

（三）"十四夜，间间亮"的故事

台州有"十四夜，间间亮"的习俗，据说也起源于戚继光抗击倭寇的故事。

明朝年间，倭寇侵扰中国沿海地区，时任参将的戚继光联合军民抗击倭寇。有一天，戚继光得知倭寇要在正月十四晚上偷袭台州

县城，于是，预先将部队埋伏在城内外各处，以给倭寇一个措手不及。同时，他又号召台州县城的每家每户准备蜡烛，一旦战斗打响，百姓家里点燃蜡烛。后来，倭寇被打败了，在县城里四处逃窜。戚继光率军追击，因为每家每户都点着蜡烛，每间房屋灯火通明，倭寇没有地方躲藏，最终被全部擒住。

为了庆祝戚家军打击倭寇的胜利，从此，台州百姓就传承了"十四夜，间间亮"的庆祝习俗。每到正月十四晚上，家家户户点上灯火，挂上彩灯，同时，主人外出赏灯时，可以防小偷偷盗。

（四）仙居针刺无骨花灯

台州人挂灯在正月十三、十四开始，一般会挂三五天。花灯中最具地方特色的要数仙居的针刺无骨花灯、黄岩橘灯等。

相传，唐朝年间，有一个仙居皤滩的秀才，有一天在夜

○仙居针刺无骨花灯

间行走时迷了路，这个时候一个善心的仙女手持"神灯"给秀才引路。回家以后，秀才把遇到的事情告诉妻子，秀才夫妇为了感谢仙女，就制作了一盏工艺独特、造型别致的灯笼，后来广泛流传于民间。

仙居针刺无骨花灯的工艺源自唐代，当地民间又称为"唐灯"，素有"中华第一灯"的美称。这种灯整个不见一根骨架，只用大小不等、形状各异的纸张粘贴接合，再把全用绣花针刺出的各种花纹图案的纸片盖上，经13道精细工序制作而成。

（五）黄岩橘灯

传说，南宋建炎年间（公元1127年—1130年），北方的金人入侵，康王赵构从海上逃走，途径浙江台州。那天刚好是正月十五，他晚上登上金鳌山观海，忽然隐约见到澄江上飘来无数灯火，感到十分奇怪，

○做橘灯

让侍从赶紧去查看真相。侍从回来后告诉赵构，说那是橘灯。赵构后来亲自来到江边观看，要求侍从一起凑热闹，买来了两船橘子。先取出橘肉让大家吃了，剩下的橘壳来制作橘灯，让橘灯顺水漂流。

此后，每到正月十五，黄岩城里的市民就来到澄江边上看橘灯漂流。

（六）吃糟羹

在中国元宵节，通常要吃汤圆，预示家庭和睦、团团圆圆，而台州过元宵节时则不吃汤圆，而是吃羹。羹制作过程比较复杂：由一大锅原料搅成一锅羹，糟羹的主材料是米粉，配上猪肉、玉米粒、豆腐干、冬笋、蚕豆、芥菜、香菇、芋头、油泡等。首先把以上原料切成丁，然后放到锅里翻炒，再加水煮熟后加入面粉，用铲子不断搅和，最后调味出锅。

○糟羹

台州吃糟羹的习俗有一个故事。相传在唐朝初

年，台州常常遭海盗烧杀抢夺，时任台州刺史的尉迟就发动兵士筑墙防盗。开工时，正是正月十四，百姓准备闹元宵，海盗也正好这天在台州湾登陆。尉迟知道这个消息后，一方面派兵抗击海盗，一方面加紧修筑城墙。当晚是元宵节之夜，风雨交加，兵士在寒冷的天气中修筑城墙的进度很慢。台州百姓们聚在一起商议，准备什么夜点慰劳筑城的兵士。有人说："送些酒和菜去吧，吃了可以御寒。"有人回答道："刺史规定在这特殊的时期，兵士不能饮酒。"就在乡亲们七嘴八舌议论时，有个人想出了一个好办法。他说："我们用糟酒当水，调进好菜和粉，搅成糟羹，这样又好吃又御寒。"乡亲们听了拍手称好，分头准备糟羹的原料，动手制作了一桶桶香飘飘的糟羹，送到筑城的兵士们跟前。兵士们喝了糟羹以后，不仅填饱了肚子，身体也随之暖和起来，干活有劲了，筑城的速度也大大加快了。在这寒冷的元宵之夜，在这危急关头，军民同心，城墙很快筑好，保护了城内百姓的安全。

　　为了纪念在元宵之夜打击海盗的胜利，台州百姓吃糟糠的习俗就流传下来。

二、
苏南水乡元宵节

苏州胜浦乡前戴村世代生长着以稻作生产为主的农民，元宵节不吃汤圆，而吃"塘草泥"，不张灯结彩，却要"踩田角落"。

（一）吃"塘草泥"

元宵节晚餐时，前戴村有吃"塘草泥"的习俗。"塘草泥"是什么呢？是当地人在濒临河边的地方，先挖一个小塘，然后将准备好的青草铺在小塘里，每铺一层草，就泼洒一些粪肥和垃圾，再浇上一层河泥，再铺一层草，撒肥浇河泥。这样一层层铺浇完毕后，用泥土封好。经过一个月的发酵，成为秧田的好基肥，当地人就把这种配料称为"塘草泥"。前戴村人在元宵节上所吃的"塘草泥"，是将过年吃剩的年糕切成块，与面条、青菜、荠菜煮在一起，看上去黏黏糊糊的，在外观上与垃圾、粪肥、青草和河泥搅和在一起的塘草泥有些相似，因此把这种混合在一起煮的食物称作"塘草泥"。吃时先献灶君和祖先，然后全家人一起吃。"塘草泥"有甜有咸，吃起来别有一番风味。

（二）踩田角落

　　人们吃过"塘草泥"后，要举行"踩田角落"活动。夜幕降临，人们或抱或挑着稻草，领着孩子来到自家田边。他们点燃稻草火把，火红的火把照亮了漆黑的夜空，也照亮了田间崎岖的小路。人们沿着田边一边奔跑，一边高喊："踩踩田角落，来年能收一千六；踩踩田角落，来年养个大猡猡（猪猡）"。烧完一束稻草，接着点上另一束，继续奔跑与高喊。每到一个田角落，要把火把放在田角落烧尽。村民们说："踩田角落可以知道今年收成的好坏，如果稻草火把燃烧的火头是红色，预示今年干，收成好；如果火头是淡红色，白烊烊的，则预示今年水大，收成不好。"这也是家家户户都踩田角落、祈求粮食盛产和丰收的原因。

　　踩完田角落后，人们要将火把从田间带回家里，首先到住宅的基地上踩一踩，这样家里就会没有毒气，住宅和家人都平安。再到猪圈、鸡鸭巢附近踩一踩，一边踩，一边高喊："踩踩猡猡圈，猡猡养得壮"；"踩踩鸡鸭巢，鸡鸭养得好"。特别引人注目的是踩水码头。前戴村每家都有一、两个水码头，是他们平时用来淘米、洗菜、洗衣服的地方。据说踩了水码头，落水鬼不会拖小孩下水、小孩不会被淹死。这些地方踩完后，人们才把燃烧的火把放进灶膛里，元宵节的踩田角落才算结束。

三、
东北元宵节送灯习俗

在辽宁的辽阳县、海城市、凤城市以及辽东地区，吉林省的通化县、梨树县等以及黑龙江省的桦川县等地，流传着元宵节送灯的习俗。元宵送灯，是在元宵节这天，给自家的祖坟送去灯盏，以示子孙尽孝、家里后世有人。在黑龙江一些地方，到了元宵节，家家户户都要做面灯，灯的形状像碗，俗称灯碗。做成碗形后，放在锅里蒸熟，插上用棉絮缠裹的芦苇做成的灯芯，在面灯碗里面倒满灯油。

○元宵节给祖先"送灯"

133

然后依次把这些面灯送到祖宗灵位、天地、灶君神位，送到仓库、牛马圈、井台、碾磨坊、送到大门旁、大路口等处。

节日中，还要把面灯送到自家已故先人的坟头上。送灯时，要赶早，越先点燃就代表越吉利，而且点灯还需用自家的火柴，如果用别人的，有祖先会看不见光明这一说法。

辽东、辽南一带的大连、丹东、营口等地区，也有送灯的习俗，但是现在大多已经用红色的蜡烛代替面灯了。元宵节期间，每当夜幕降临，家里的男人就带着纸钱和灯，来到自家坟地里，首先给先辈烧纸钱，然后点燃蜡烛，即为送灯。回家的路上每逢十字路口，都要点上一支蜡烛。女人则在家里给灶台、猪圈、井口、粮仓点上蜡烛。当地人说："在坟地里送灯是给老祖宗照亮抓虱子；在十字路口点蜡烛送灯，是为了让老祖宗回家过灯节时能找到路。送灯还有送'丁'之意，希望老祖宗能保佑全家人丁兴旺。"

○面灯

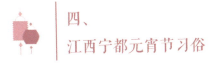

四、
江西宁都元宵节习俗

江西宁都县各乡镇的闹元宵活动，特色鲜明。

（一）石上村"添丁炮"

在石上村，最隆重的习俗就是元宵节的"添丁炮"。每年正月十四、十五两日，凡在这一年生育男孩的家庭都要举行传统的燃放"添丁炮"与"割鸡"仪式。头年生育男孩家里的亲戚朋友会送来

○石上村的"添丁炮"仪式

135

一大串爆竹，集中放在家族祠堂前。孩子的外婆家还要请唢呐锣鼓队助兴。下午，在老街的汉帝庙举行"割鸡"仪式，所有添丁的人家都会集中在这里，按抽签的顺序到汉帝庙割鸡朝拜。仪式结束后，舞龙队进行表演。然后，所有添丁的人家要按照规定的路线，一路上鸣鞭放炮、敲锣打鼓，到祖宗祠堂拜祖，告慰先人。下午四点后，祠堂前的爆竹同时点燃，震耳欲聋的爆竹声冲天而起，场面尤为壮观，表达了村民对添丁的喜悦。

（二）曾坊村"桥梆灯"

村里只要有人家去年生了孩子，不管男女，也不管是第一胎还是第二胎，都要列入扎制"桥梆灯"的行列。另外，哪一家去年娶了新媳妇进门，今年元宵节也要扎"桥梆灯"。"桥梆灯"是在一根长4.5米左右的"桥梆"上，扎十盏架子灯，灯座上有安放蜡烛的座孔，灯架用白纸贴封，白纸上贴有红色的剪纸。村里有多少人添丁，就扎多少排"桥梆灯"。例如去年曾坊村增添了20个人，就要扎20排"桥梆灯"。夜幕降临，几十名壮年男子抬着"桥梆灯"开始巡游活动。整个队伍犹如一条火龙，龙头与龙尾进行各种队形变化与表演。

○曾坊村"桥梆灯"

活动通常进行几个小时，让观众看个尽兴，方告结束。

（三）大布村"兔子灯"

大布村有一项古老的民俗叫"过灯"。在当地有这样的传说：明朝万历年间，大布村有一位姓罗的商人，在扬州时，迷上了"兔子灯""扛灯"的工艺。于是，装成哑巴拜师学艺，通过三年的辛勤学习，才学会了这门制作灯彩的技艺。他回到了大布村，并把这项技艺陆续传授给村民。

"兔子灯"是一种集体活动。每年正月初十至十五的晚上，是"过灯"的日子，也是大布村热闹的日子。在5000多人的大布村，每家每户都要扎一盏一母二仔抱成团的"兔子灯"。灯由三个并

○大布村兔子灯

列的兔子头组成，中间的兔子稍大，是兔婆，旁边二盏是小兔子。"兔子灯"用竹篾做骨架，以红、绿、白三色纸糊贴。兔身里安放一碗用茶油浸泡的白米，米中间放灯芯草，巡游时就点燃灯芯。

活动开始时，在响彻云天的锣鼓唢呐声中，由近千人组成的游灯队伍浩浩荡荡走家过户，穿街过巷、巡游在田埂上、池塘边，最后聚集在祠堂里。之后，村里人还会按家族分别到事先议定好的人家里热闹一番，这些人家都是年前有喜事的。主人家则要备好茶点酒席来招待这些贺喜的乡亲，因为"兔子灯"队伍的到来，象征着乡亲们给家里送来了吉祥如意的好运气。连续几天，大布村人都沉浸在欢乐喜庆之中。

（四）江背村"扛灯"

"扛灯"是流传在宁都的一种客家民俗。在石上镇江背村，有这样一个传说：有一个菩萨叫"杨氏婆婆"，是当地的一个守护神。村民们在村里建了一栋"慈恩阁"来纪念她，十里乡亲也都喜欢到这位"杨氏婆婆"面前去许愿求福。只要哪家许的愿应验了，这家人就要到"杨氏婆婆"面前去还愿。有的人许的愿比较大，就要制作花灯，这就是"扛灯"的由来。当地的另一说法是：江背村人尊崇汉帝王，自村里建起了汉帝庙后，特别制作了一种灯饰，叫作"扛灯"，用来在节日里拜谒汉王时，进行游灯活动。

正月十四晚，江背村的"扛灯"活动如期举行。精致的花灯云集在"慈恩阁"供人欣赏，再游向村里的每个角落。这种灯有四层，高达 1.8 米左右，围宽 1.3 米。它的外观全部用各种精美的花样剪纸裱糊，有古代的才子佳人、神话故事人物、名花贵树、百鸟动物等图案。"扛灯"装扮得花红柳绿，美轮美奂。"扛灯"内设有 20 多只油碗，游村时，就把所有油碗灯点亮。凭借火的热能，推动灯饰上的各种图像自行转动，整个"扛灯"就会呈现出一幅幅动画般的美丽画面。同时，在游灯活动中，还有不少的菩萨轿及鼓乐队，排成阵阵长龙，徐徐跟进。游灯时，村里还会点放土铳，家家户户燃放鞭炮，以示庆贺。晚上村里还请戏班唱戏，整个村里热闹非凡，节日气氛十分浓郁。

（五）进贤元宵鸡子

元宵鸡子是用大米做原料加工成米团，再以手工捏造而成的象形制品。自古以来，进贤的百姓都将其作为元宵节食品或者祭祀贡品一代代沿袭下来。在江西很多地方，民间用碗装白米素食，再插上筷子作为贡品，很少有米塑贡品，所以显得异常珍贵。元宵节时，米塑贡品多以鸡的形象出现，尽管还有猪、狗、猴、龙、鱼、家禽等其他丰富的物象表现，进贤人还是直观地统称这类米制的象形制

多彩中国节

元宵节

品为元宵鸡子。米塑制品中，还有不少用柏树枝与鸡子或蛋组合捏制的"发财树"、"摇钱树"。

远古时期，鸟被视为"日精"，是太阳和男性的象征，是人类繁衍之神。鸡作为鸟的变体或替代物，有生殖的寓意。于是，鸡的形象被供奉在宗族祠堂或先灵佛龛前，以体现后人对生命的敬畏，对祖先的感恩。同时，鸡能报晓黎明，唤醒大地，是报晨报春的吉祥之鸟。元宵节之际，进贤地区将鸡奉为神灵供奉的习俗自古以来代代相传。

元宵鸡子保质期较短，制作早了容易干裂、颜色变暗淡。在当地，一般正月初十下午开始准备制作材料，磨米、打浆、湿粉染色等制作一直要持续到正月十二。多数人则是在正月十三、十四当天凌晨制作，往往米团蒸出来后，饱满而光亮。

五、
台湾：火树银花闹元宵

（一）平溪天灯

平溪乡放灯活动有悠久的历史，如今，一年比一年隆重，天灯数量越来越多，体积越来越大。灯上绘有各种精美的图案，写上放

○平溪天灯

灯者的姓名，在当地有"灯放得越高，事业做得越旺"的说法。

　　天灯又称为"孔明灯"。相传，三国时期，诸葛孔明被司马懿围困于阳平，无法派兵出城求救。孔明算准风向后，利用热气上升的原理，制成可飘浮的纸灯笼，使灯盏飘浮在空中，系上求救的讯息。援军看到后速来支援，诸葛大军脱险。于是后世就称这种灯笼为"孔明灯"。

　　平溪放天灯的习俗始于清朝道光年间。先民由大陆福建省惠安、安溪等县渡海移民到台湾的台北县、新北市平溪乡等地区开垦。据平溪乡十分地区的老人讲：道光年间，十分地区常有盗匪骚扰聚落，村民只好到山中避难。待土匪走后，

○放天灯

留守在村中的壮丁在夜间向空中施放天灯作为信号，告知山上避难的村民可以安全返乡。由于村民从山上避难回家的当天正是农历正月十五元宵节，从此以后，每年元宵节，十分地区的村民便以放天灯的仪式来庆祝节日，且向邻村的村民互报平安。十分地区的村民又称天灯为"祈福灯"或"平安灯"。现在放天灯已经成为祈福纳喜的活动，吸引了众多人前往平溪乡参与节日的盛会。

（二）盐水蜂炮

在台湾，有"南蜂炮，北天灯"之说 。这里的"南蜂炮"，指的就是台南县盐水镇元宵夜的著名习俗。

盐水镇蜂炮的习俗始于清朝。相传，清朝光绪十一年（公元1885年）的夏天，盐水地区发生了百年不遇的鼠疫，上千名村民患病而死亡。地方民众面对瘟疫束手无策，只能祈求神灵降临。农历正月十三，是关圣帝君的生日，村民就在这天迎请关老爷入境驱邪，并设计了如蜂窝般的"蜂炮"助阵，以期把瘟神吓走。应请的"神轿"从武庙出发，绕境祈求平安。"神轿"所到之处，烟火鞭炮齐放。由正月十三至十五，一连三天，全城经过硫黄硝烟彻底洗礼后，瘟疫终于驱除。百姓为了感谢关圣帝君神灵保佑，从此便在每年的元宵节连续燃放三天的蜂炮以感谢神恩，祈求村民健康平安。

当地的另一种说法是：盐水镇村民面对无可奈何的瘟疫，祈求神灵庇护。后来关圣帝君降旨绕境降魔，指示元宵夜由周仓将军为前导，关帝神轿压阵护队，村中信徒们跟随到后面，并且绕着疫区行走。沿路上一直燃放蜂炮直到天亮。绕境结束后，盐水镇的瘟疫竟然消除了。民众为了感谢神恩，从此每年元宵节都燃放爆竹，逐渐演变今天的蜂炮盛会。

因为"蜂炮"起源于祈福，所以盐水人认为，经历"蜂炮"越多，洗礼越多，来年便更顺利平安。虽然每年放"蜂炮"花费不菲，但祈望新年风调雨顺、平安无病也值得。现在"蜂炮"已成为一项地方风俗，每年吸引不少观光客，盐水小镇也因此闻名。

对盐水镇来说，正月十五是当之无愧的"蜂狂"之夜，以惊险刺激而著称，台湾各地民众云集盐水镇，目睹热闹的蜂炮盛会。观看放"蜂炮"，一定要头戴安全帽、嘴戴口

○ 盐水蜂炮

罩、手戴手套、穿长外套，甚至要带橡皮筋，系在裤脚，以防"蜂炮"从脚下袭来，钻进裤管爆开。"蜂狂"夜，"蜂炮"发出宛如蜂鸣的声响，数以万计的爆竹宛如蜂群倾巢而出。此起彼伏的鞭炮声，不时爆开的灿烂烟花，让平静的小镇增添了节日的喜庆。对于"蜂炮"，被炸到者都不会生气，因为被炸到得越多，也就越有福气。盐水镇人相信炮仗做得越大，蜂炮做得越多，来年的生意就会越旺盛。

（三）台东炮炸寒单爷

位于台湾东南部的台东是全岛人口最少的一个县，但元宵节期间的"炮炸寒单爷"习俗名扬全岛。关于"寒单爷"，由于历史口耳相传中所造成的误传，名称又有"寒丹、韩单、韩丹、韩郸、邯郸、邯丹、邯单"等多种写法。很多民俗学者认为"寒单"应是"玄坛"的讹音造成。早期台湾元宵节庆祝活动中所特有的"迎玄坛爷"游街习俗应当是"炸寒单爷"。

关于寒单爷的来历，有三个传说故事。其一，寒单爷又称"玄坛元帅"。玄坛爷出自封神榜，本名是赵公明，曾是商朝时期鲁国（今

山东）终南山人，任武官。武王伐纣的时候，协助闻太师抵御周军的进攻，后来被姜子牙用法术所杀。功德圆满后，赵公明成为司职禳灾保安、买卖生财之神。在封神榜上，受封为"金龙如意正一龙虎玄坛真君"，又称"银主公王"，俗称"武财神"。其二，据说寒单爷是所谓的"流氓神"。他曾是地方上的一大恶霸，名叫韩单，专门欺压弱小乡民。某一天，他得到了神佛的感化指点，于是大彻大悟、痛改前非。他站上软轿，让乡民们用火炮炸他，直到死去为止。其三，乡民对恶霸韩单的欺压忍无可忍，遂假借元宵节宴请韩单，把他灌醉，并投鞭炮将他炸死。三个传说中，与节日习俗关系最紧密的是第一个。

在台东等地，每年正月十五，寒爷出巡，一连两天，伴随着各路神明绕境。据说寒单爷生性怕冷，每当寒单爷出巡时，民众就投鞭炮为他驱寒，因此就有了"炮炸寒单爷"的说法。另一方面，人们相信他为商朝武将，不惧水火。此外，也有向财神爷求财之意。像台东及花莲的"炮炸寒单爷"、竹南中港的"迎寒单"、盐水的蜂炮谢神恩等活动，都有"愈放愈发""愈炸愈发"的涵义。节日中，以真人装扮的寒单爷赤裸上身，画上大花脸、头系红帽巾，站在用藤制成的藤椅上，这种藤椅一般称为"椅轿"或"软轿"，不同于一般神明出巡时所乘坐之神轿。寒单爷出巡称为"走佛"或"烧佛"。出巡时，寒单爷仅拿一把榕叶护体。所到之处，民众热烈地用鞭炮去炸，爆竹震耳欲聋，而寒单爷面不改色，神气活现。四处飞蹿的鞭炮在"寒单爷"身边爆炸，场面刺激，扣人心弦，引来观众们不断的尖叫声。民众鞭炮炸得越旺，

○炸寒单爷

代表财运就越发。

目前在台湾供奉寒单爷的地方，除了主要盛行地台东以外，还有花莲的行德宫、玉里的金阙堂、台东寒单爷恒春分堂、北港"武德宫"及桃园、宜兰头城、苗栗竹南中港等地，但真有肉身寒单接受炮炸的仅在台东。

（四）澎湖"乞龟"

"乞龟"是澎湖元宵节最具地方特色的民俗文化活动，也是台湾地区特有的一个盛大民间习俗。龟是灵物，千年生毛，寿五千岁，称为神龟，万年则称为灵龟。元宵节时，台湾各寺庙常举办"乞龟"活动。位于台湾海峡中的澎湖县马公天后宫的"乞龟"活动最具规模，最为盛行。

"乞龟"意即乞求神明赐龟，是流传久远的传统民俗，迄今不断。"乞龟"最早起源于无嗣妇人求子。据清代举人林豪著《澎湖厅志》引清朝澎湖通判胡建伟著《澎湖纪略》记载："各庙中张灯，男女出

○澎湖"乞龟"

游看灯。庙中扎有花卉、人物，男妇有求嗣者，在神前祈杯，求得花一枝或面龟一个，回家供奉。如果添丁，则明年元宵时，倍数酬谢。"经过100多年的演化，"乞龟"已不再单单只是民众求子的一种寄托，更多的是祈求平安、健康或财利。由于70%以上的澎湖人是泉州移民，而泉州的"乞龟"风俗源远流长，"乞龟祈福"民俗可能就是百年以前由泉州传到澎湖，移民们在澎湖保留并延续了这一风俗。

　　早年用的是真正的龟，后来由于环保和动物保护等原因，才改成了现在的米龟。"乞龟"，最初是由寺庙提供面龟、红毛龟等寿龟（一种龟形的糕点），供信徒掷筊乞赐。待得到神明的允赐后，信徒就可以把面龟带回家，保全家平安或用来祈求贵子。过去，"乞龟"的方法十分简单，有意愿的民众可以前往任何庙宇，相中庙里罗列的众多小神龟之一，燃上三炷清香敬告神明，然后掷杯请示神明获准。如获成杯（一阴一阳），则将香插在龟背以示"名龟有主"，并向庙方登记后，迎回家中供奉三天后再分切食用。唯一条件是明年元宵节必须定做一只送回庙里酬谢，而且分量必须大于今年乞走的那一只。澎湖"乞龟"还有个有趣的习俗：凡"乞"得"龟"或其他的供品，回家的路上不可与人说话，即便遇到好朋友也只能点头微笑，否则据说会使乞得的心愿半路流失。乞得之物带回家后，通常供奉三天。如果乞到的是个"大龟"，必须敲锣打鼓运回家，供在家里，让人参观。期间须每天上香参拜。仪式过后，可将得"大龟"拆散，分送亲友或乡民"吃平安"，唯独"龟"的头部不能施予，以保留自家的祈愿而自享。下一年的元宵节，还愿者须按庙宇张榜公布的数目订制供品，提前送往庙中。如奉还的是"大龟"，还须敲锣打鼓鸣鞭炮，在神前三跪九叩，以完成还愿的礼仪。乞得米龟的信徒如果事业得意或家中求得儿女后，必须准备加重的米龟供其他信徒求乞。由于龟是长寿吉祥的象征，再加上是神明的赐予，所以深受民众的喜爱，成为

145

一项热闹有趣的元宵节民俗活动。

　　每年元宵节，澎湖群岛居民就推出"乞龟"寺庙活动。这时，澎湖全县各家各户都悬挂宫灯，各寺庙供乞的大小龟多达千只以上，种类繁多。为了吸引信徒，各庙宇无不费尽心思、出奇制胜，纷纷在材质、大小方面设计出独特的龟族样式。同时，乞龟活动更具多样化，例如举行大游行，并有神轿队、民俗队及民乐演奏队加入阵容。

　　以前，澎湖制作的米龟一般都要用 10 斤、20 斤米，近年来，由于生活水平有所提高，一年做得比一年大，所以上千斤的米龟也经常有。同时，元宵节可供祈求的"龟种"物品种类愈来愈多，除面龟、肉龟、糯米龟、巧克力龟、面线龟、麻薯龟、黑糖龟、蛋糕龟、果冻龟、米龟、糖果龟之外，还有金钱龟、黄金龟等，让元宵乞平安龟的祈福活动更具特色。

　　现在，澎湖举行"乞龟"活动规模较大的有寺庙包括马公镇天后宫、东边的隘门三圣殿、南端的山水上帝庙、锁港北极殿、赤龙德宫和外垵温王庙。每年，"乞龟"的人数都不少，有的家族甚至派出多人接力参赛，志在必得。

（五）野柳"洗港祭"

　　每年元宵节，在台北市万里乡野柳村的保安宫，有一项特别的活动叫作"洗港祭"。这个习俗也有一个传说：早年，开漳圣王陈元光因为智勇双全、知人善任而享誉闽奥，在唐朝先天元年由武则天赐其"忠毅文惠"谥号。有一天，他通过乩童（乩童是一种职业，类似西方的灵媒，是道教仪式中，神明跟人或鬼魂跟人之间的媒介）告诉村民，自己要在正月十五元宵节这天去港口洗一洗尘埃。此后每年元宵节，野柳乡民都会恭请当地保安宫的开漳圣王、天上圣母、周仓将军以及土地公等诸神，到渔港中净港。

146

每年到了元宵节这天，当地百姓准备好祭品。首先恭请四神上轿，然后再由四个壮汉抬起神轿在村内绕境游行。接下来，连人带轿跃入渔港边的浅海中，进行"洗港"，最后登上对岸，举行"过火"仪式，祈求村民平安与丰收。仪式中，先由道士祷告，祈求神明护佑本次"过火"平安顺利。然后将草席在火堆四周挥舞，再将米和盐撒入炭火中。之后，抬轿的四名壮汉反复在火堆上来回跑，一边跑一边口中念念有词。片刻后，道士发出指令，神轿开始过火。随后，身体有病或有求于神明的信徒也纷纷冲过火堆，用赤脚在炭火上走过，以得到神灵庇佑。据说神明在经过"过火"仪式洗礼后，可洗尽邪气污染，再度发挥神力，保佑村民。"过火"仪式后，神轿在信徒们的簇拥下在野柳的大街小巷内巡行以驱赶邪魔。神轿游行完毕后返回保安宫，整个"洗港""过火"仪式结束。

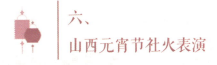

六、
山西元宵节社火表演

社火是中国中原地区古老的民间艺术形式，指在祭祀或节日里迎神会上各种杂戏、杂耍的表演，也是高台、高跷、旱船、舞狮、舞龙、秧歌等表演的统称。"社"，古代指土地神，"火"，即火神，社火来源于古代人们对土地与火的崇拜。

147

关于社火有一个神话故事：相传水神共工的儿子勾龙是社神。共工长得人脸蛇身，满头红发，性格暴烈好战。有一天，他和火神祝融作战，一怒之下头触不周山（不周山为古代传说中的山名，即今昆仑山西北部的帕米尔。相传不周山是人界唯一能够到达天界的路径，但不周山终年寒冷，长年飘雪，一般人很难徒步到达），竟把撑天的柱子碰断。顿时天崩地裂，洪水泛滥。这时多亏女娲炼了五彩石及时把天补好。勾龙见父亲闯下大祸，心里非常难过，于是把九州大裂缝一一填平。黄帝见状，便封他为"后土"，让他丈量并掌管土地。从此勾龙便成为人们祭祀的社神。

（一）晋中社火

在山西晋中，流传着一句谚语："老百姓，要快活，赶会唱戏弄红火。"在晋中过年，社火活动从正月初一持续到正月十五元宵节才算结束。元宵节是晋中社火中灯火最旺、歌舞最多的高潮时期。晋

○山西社火表演

中的社火按照表演形式可分为锣鼓类、秧歌类、车船轿类、灯火类、模拟禽兽类、模拟鬼神类等。锣鼓类，表演节奏强烈明快、场面壮阔粗犷；秧歌类，有的侧重歌唱，有的歌舞结合，以舞为主；车船轿类，用道具装扮成民间交通工具；灯火类，继承传统灯火艺术，又结合地方文化特色；模拟禽兽类以及模拟鬼神类，表现远古时期人类与自然界凶猛禽兽的斗争，反映人类对妖魔鬼怪的迷信与敬畏。

（二）左权"串火盘"

在左权县的社火上，最精彩的活动是元宵节晚上的"串火盘"。这里的"火盘"，其实是在乡民自家或者商铺门口点燃的"旺火"。用大块煤炭垒成一个塔状，里面放木柴。旺火燃起后吐着火

○山西社火节

舌，红光耀眼，恰似一条吞云吐火的飞龙，被认为能给人们带来吉祥如意。方圆百里的人都要赶来观看旺火，以图吉利，有的人还要围着最大的"旺火"绕三圈，以图全家平安。这种旺火矮的一米多，高的二三米。元宵节时，文艺队或说唱的能手就在"旺火"旁表演歌舞、武术等具有地方特色的节目。当地人认为："参加'串火盘'表演能给来年带来好运，于是大家一边烤火，一边欣赏传统节目，既热闹又喜庆。"从前，"串火盘"是为了给商铺或个人招揽人气，讨个好彩头，从而得到烟酒等报酬。如今，"串火盘"成为左权县群众性的欢庆活动。

（三）平遥元宵节

在古城平遥，保存了浓郁的元宵节地方文化，其中的"社社"求"子"归、游驾高跷舞、道备"游黄河阵"最具特色。

"社社"是一座小庙，里面供着"送子娘娘"。有"社社"的村中，由村民轮流当值"社社"。轮到当值的人家在正月十三就要打开"社社"的门，把里面清扫干净，挂上红灯。还要到各家各户去"起钱"，用来买一些泥娃娃、红枣、花生、核桃、柿饼等。正月十五早上，家中的儿媳妇如果还未怀孕，婆婆们就准备东西去"社社"贡献，她们烧香、磕头，祈求"送子娘娘"保佑儿媳妇早日怀孕。之后会请一个"扳不倒"回家，再拿一些红枣、花生等回家。而有些村庄，并不是由婆婆去请"扳不倒"，是由闹红火的队伍于当日傍晚"送子"回家。一是这样做更加红火喜庆，二是人们可以借机瞧一瞧别人家不常出门的新媳妇。

游驾是平遥南政乡所辖的自然村，分为东游驾村与西游驾村。游驾最出名的是高跷，在正月十四至十六间会去附近的其他村子演出。整个表演不仅规模较大，而且内容丰富，艺术形式有趣。表演开始时，前面是敲钹为主的乐队，后面跟着三四十架踩高跷的队伍。踩高跷者都穿着戏服，有扮相俊俏的小媳妇，也有像猪八戒一样的丑八怪。在钹声的伴奏下，高跷队伍沿街有节奏地进行表演，表情夸张，扭捏的动作不时引来两旁观众的欢笑。在过去，高跷队伍还要去大户人家表演，最惊险的画面是，地上放条长木桌，然后高跷一架架依次瞬间跨越过去，主人随后递上"顺风烟"与零钱酬谢。

道备村也属于南政乡，距平遥古城北仅 10 公里。道

○社火游驾表演

多彩中国节

元宵节

备村元宵节最热闹的节目要数"游黄河阵"。村里有一块足球场大小的空地,元宵节前,村民用高粱秆搭建成一个约 10,000 平方米的"迷宫"。迷宫的"墙"约有 1 米多高,间隔 1 米～2 米的墙上就挂一盏灯。迷宫里曲折环绕,有多个进口,但是只有从其中的一个进口进去才能找到出口,其他进口进去都走不出来。另外,即使从正确的进口入内,里面还有多个岔道,一不小心,就会迷失方向。这个迷宫名叫"黄河",寓黄河九曲十八弯。"游黄河阵"必须在正月十六举行,当地也叫作"游百病"。人们希望通过游迷宫,全年百病祛除,身体健康。

旅游小贴士

山西平遥古城

平遥古城位于山西省中部平遥县内,是中国境内保存最为完整的一座古代县城,基本保存了明清时期县城的原型,有"龟城"之称。街道格局为"土"字形,建筑布局则遵从八卦的方位,体现了明清

○平遥古城

时的城市规划理念和形制分布。城内外有各类遗址、古建筑300多处，有保存完整的明清民宅近4000座，街道商铺都体现历史原貌，被称作研究中国古代城市的活样本，在中国历史的发展中，为人们展示了一幅非同寻常的文化、社会、经济及宗教发展的完整画卷。

平遥旧称"古陶"，明朝初年，为防御外族南扰，始建城墙，洪武三年（公元1370年）在旧墙垣基础上重筑扩修，并全面包砖。以后景泰、正德、嘉靖、隆庆和万历各代进行过十次的补修，更新城楼，增设敌台。康熙四十三年（公元1703年）因皇帝西巡路经平遥，而在城四面筑了四座大城楼，使城池更加壮观。平遥城墙总周长6163米，墙高约12米，把面积约2.25平方公里的平遥县城一隔为两个风格迥异的世界。城墙以内街道、铺面、市楼保留明清形制；城墙以外称新城。这是一座古代与现代建筑各成一体、交相辉映、令人遐思不已的佳地。

交通：从太原乘火车到平遥火车站，步行、在火车站乘坐观光车或出租车便可到平遥古城；或到太原建南汽车站坐乘大巴车直达平遥汽车站，步行即可到平遥古城。

门票价格：平遥古城景点联票130元。

著名景点：明清一条街、平遥县衙博物馆。

建议游玩时长：1—2天。

适宜游玩季节：四季皆宜。

七、
山东元宵节习俗

（一）逛庙会

在山东各地，元宵节期间的庙会是比较热闹的活动。其中以蓬莱阁庙会最具典型性。

蓬莱，是中国神话故事中八仙过海的起程点，自古就有崇尚神

○蓬莱阁庙会

仙的习俗。蓬莱阁庙会已有百余年历史。相传，正月十六是天后海神娘娘的生日，所以蓬莱人有了正月十六赶庙会的习俗。现在，一年一度的庙会已经发展成为蓬莱市传统的节日民俗盛会。每年都有来自周边和全国各地近万名群众前来蓬莱阁烧香拜佛，观光游玩。游人们在蓬莱阁戏楼、广场上观看戏曲、秧歌等表演，品尝地方美食，蓬莱阁上人山人海、热闹非凡。正月十三、十四，渔民们则要过"渔灯节"，人们纷纷到蓬莱阁的龙王宫送灯、进奉贡品，祈求龙王爷保佑新的一年出海平安和渔业丰收。

旅游小贴士

蓬 莱 阁

蓬莱地处山东半岛最北端，濒临渤海、黄海，北距辽东半岛66海里。东与韩国、日本隔海相望，海岸线长86公里，全市总面积1200平方公里。蓬莱素有"仙境"之誉，它依山傍海，景色秀丽，独具虚无缥缈的"海市蜃楼"奇观。蓬莱是山东历史文化名城。有历代名胜古迹100余处。建于宋嘉祐六年(公元1061年)的蓬莱阁和建于宋庆历二年(公元1042年)的蓬莱水城均为国家重点文物保护单位。其中，蓬莱阁是中国古代四大名楼之一，是凝聚着古代汉族劳动人民智慧和艺术结晶的古建群，由弥陀寺、龙王宫、子孙殿、天后宫、三清殿、吕祖殿等古建筑共同构成，占地32 800平方米，建筑面积18 960平方米，楼亭殿阁分布得宜，建筑园林交相辉映，各因地势，协调壮观。蓬莱阁主阁建于山顶，远远望去，楼亭殿阁掩映在绿树丛中，高踞山崖之上，恍如神话中的仙宫。

交通：从烟台莱山机场乘出租车到烟台长途车站，坐烟蓬旅游快车到蓬莱汽车站，下车往西步行五分钟到蓬莱阁振扬门售票处。

门票：通票140元。

最佳游玩时节：7月－9月。

（二）赏花灯

逛灯会也是山东元宵节期间必不可少的活动。在济南，每逢元宵节，在趵突泉全省各地的大型花灯队要进行表演。其他地方灯会也是流光溢彩，著名的有泰安岱庙灯会、烟台山灯谜迎春会、淄博奎盛园民间艺术花灯会、东营黄河口元宵灯会、聊城阳谷狮子楼元宵灯会、日照烟花灯会、莱芜元宵节花灯会等。

山东各地的元宵花灯，大致可以分为"静态灯"与"动态灯"

○赏花灯

两大类。静态灯有壁灯、立灯、吊灯等，多放置于建筑物上。动态灯的形式较为丰富，一种是手提灯，灯上配一长杆，可以提着走街串巷。淮县城里小孩喜欢的"老猫灯"颇具特色。"老猫灯"的外形并不是猫的形象，而是麒麟的样子。灯用铁丝扎制，再糊上麻纱，最后彩绘而成。分灯头、灯身、灯尾三部分，用铁丝簧连接而成，提着"老猫灯"行走时，整个灯摇头摆尾，分外生动。其他动态灯中，最常见的是龙灯，风格样式各不相同。龙灯由龙头、龙尾和少则10余节、多则30节的龙身组成。整个龙灯的彩绘只用两三种颜色，身上的麒麟片，用一种当地称为"鬼子兰"的蓝色彩绘，腹部环纹、火苗以及胡须、口唇等则为粉红、大红色，其他部位以黑色、金色及白色相间，整条龙看去非常鲜明生动。龙灯以"火珠灯"（也称蜘蛛灯）作引导。此外，作为舞具出现的彩灯还有狮子灯、航船灯、鸟兽灯、家畜灯等。腰灯也很有特色，是将灯按结构分为前后两节，分别系在人腰的前后或左右。比如毛驴灯，是按真实的比例（或略小于真实）扎制成毛驴形状。头颈、前肢及前身为一节，系在玩灯人的腰前；毛驴的尾部，后肢及后身为一节，系在玩灯人的腰后。毛驴灯的下部用布遮盖，这样玩灯的人看上去就像骑在驴背上一样。骑驴的男子化装成小媳妇的样子，起跑舞步、前俯后仰的样子十分动人。此外，还有一些供儿童玩的蝴蝶灯、金鱼灯。

山东地方文化丰富多彩，花灯的名称和寓意也各不相同。

曹县"雪花灯"。大多以细长圆直的高粱秆做成骨架，灯有四个角，表面用白纸糊好，上面镂刻有装饰图案。灯的最里层有点燃的蜡烛，烛光照在刻有镂空图案的纸上，层层叠叠，非常别致。近年来，"雪花灯"在品种、造型上均有所发展，出现了"牌坊灯""楼阁灯""马车灯""家具灯"等。

东明"年灯"。在黄河一带的东明县等地农村流行一种极富特色的观赏与食用相结合的灯彩艺术，叫作"年灯"，采用加水合好的黍子面制作而成。首先把黍子面在锅内蒸熟，揉成面团，再用手、剪刀、竹筒等工具进行捏、压等加工，再用绿豆、黑豆等装点动物的眼睛，最后做成各种艺术形式的灯彩，常见的有"十二生肖"灯。每件年灯中部有一个碗形的灯槽，用来装麻油，还有一根棉花灯芯，可供点燃。面灯点亮时，显得格外晶莹剔透。"年灯"的题材多为寓意吉祥的鸟兽，所放置位置也有讲究，如粮囤上放"刺猬灯"，是为了防鼠偷粮；饭锅里放置"鱼灯"，寓意年年有余；牲口棚里放置"牛马灯"，象征"六畜兴旺"，等等。待元宵夜过后，灯油燃尽时，人们把年灯收回，将年灯揉成面团，放在大容器里发酵，然后再做成年糕食用。

单县"河灯"。每年正月初七、十五放"河灯"。河灯分为两种，一种是悬挂在船舶上的灯，另一种是底盘用木板或竹片制成，漂浮在水面的灯。"河灯"大多数用苇草和竹篾扎成，再糊上彩纸，做成形态各异的牡丹、荷花、绣球、花瓶等。灯内装有蜡烛或油灯灯芯，可以将其点燃。夜幕降临的时候，人们纷纷来到河边放河灯，一串串河灯漂在水面上，灯光闪烁，五彩缤纷。

潍坊"老牛灯"。潍坊的元宵彩灯不仅品种繁多，而且手工精细，最有特点的是

○赏花灯

157

"老牛灯"。临近元宵佳节，当地人就在白浪河滩上扎一条七八米长的"老牛灯"，到张灯时分，引来众多民众前来观看、触摸。当地有"摸摸老牛不害眼"的民谣。此外，元宵节时，各家各户都要扎制小牛灯，一起玩耍。

（三）惠民"胡集书会"

从春节持续到元宵节的惠民县"胡集书会"，是一种曲艺集市盛会。胡集书会从元朝兴起，至清初极盛，一直沿袭至今，已有700余年的历史。最早源于曲艺艺人的竞技活动，后逐渐演变为以联谊为主、具有习俗性质的自发性民间曲艺交流活动。胡集在历史上商业发达，是方圆百余里内最大的集镇。

正月十二是春节后的第一个大集，周围群众准备欢度元宵节，纷纷前往胡集置办元宵节用品。各地说书艺人也利用这个机会，从四面八方赶到胡集，登场亮艺。说书场面热闹非凡，场面逐年扩大，形成盛大的胡集书会。

胡集书会分为前节、正节、偏节三个阶段。

○胡集书会

正月十一之前，来自本省以及各地的说书艺人，带着乐器和行李，纷纷云集胡集镇。艺人们来胡集的途中，沿途说书卖艺，称为"前节"。

正月十二大早，各路说书人来到集上，摆下摊子，扯旗

○ 胡集书会上的艺人表演

挂牌，各自登场献艺，书会正式开始。由这天一直到正月十六，为"正节"。这期间有正月十五元宵节，包括跑龙灯、扭秧歌、踩高跷、抬芯子、杂耍、武术等传统艺术表演，书会达到高潮。正节期间，艺人的演出要价最高。书会上曲种丰富多彩，有西河大鼓、木板大鼓、毛竹板书、评书、渤海大鼓、山东快书、山东琴书、渔鼓书等。胡集附近村镇的农民特别爱好听书，派出内行人到会上挑选中意的节目，再邀请艺人到本村演唱，由本村人付给报酬。从正月十二晚间起，一连几天，各村的白天和晚上都有艺人说唱。若主人挽留，艺人就继续说唱下去，若主人不留，艺人就再赶正月十七的大集书会。

从正月十七日至二十一日，称为"偏节"。偏节过后，书会才散场。

书会期间，艺人们互相拜年，切磋技艺，收徒拜师。书会散后，艺人们又沿途卖艺归去。来年正月十二，艺人们又从四面八方来到胡集相聚。

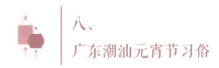

八、广东潮汕元宵节习俗

潮汕地区元宵节具有不同于其他地方的有趣习俗。

（一）吊喜灯

从正月十一到正月十八，潮汕家家户户有点灯、吊灯的习俗。因潮汕语"灯"和"丁"同音，点灯和添丁是近音，故认为点灯即为添丁的佳兆。元宵当日，人们纷纷提着灯笼、备齐纸银香烛，到庙中点火，回来分别吊在家里的神龛和床头处，叫作"吊喜灯"。

如果是去年元宵以后生了男孩子，正月十三起家人就必须挑起一对红灯笼，并在灯屏下贴红纸写上姓名，欢天喜地挂到宗族祠堂的灯架上，象征着家中添了丁。每晚家人要抱着孩子到祠堂中，一面往自己的灯笼里点燃蜡烛，使灯笼通红，一面接受周围乡人的祝贺。

○吊喜灯

吊喜灯节以正月十一

日上灯起，正月十五为中心，到正月十八日落灯止。在这段时间，城乡各地都举办丰富多彩的民俗活动，如游花灯、看新娘、办丁桌等。

（二）游花灯

潮汕元宵游花灯，历史悠久。明嘉靖刻本潮剧《荔镜记》取材于潮州民间传说。说的是明朝泉州人陈三探亲途经潮州，适逢元宵节，上街赏灯时偶遇黄五娘，两人一见钟情，经过一番波折，终成眷属的故事。至清代，潮汕游花灯更盛。清初潮州青龙庙建成后，每年安济圣王巡游时也游花灯，一连三夜，最后还要把花灯集中在一起，组织各方人士进行评比。年复一年，精益求精，使潮州花灯远近闻名。潮汕花灯屏的制作，在清末时已达到较高水平。

现在，由民间组织及各行铺出资制作花灯，晚上穿街过巷游行。花灯队伍前导为火把、龙灯，接着是潮州小锣鼓和花灯屏，末尾是一只五彩凤。潮汕花灯不同于北京的宫灯、上海的龙灯和广州的走

○游花灯

161

马灯，形式多种多样，风格独特，有纱灯、活景等。花灯题材有花果、虫鱼、鸟兽和戏剧、民间故事人物等。除了游花灯，大街小巷、行铺、院落、祠堂等也张灯结彩，挂各式各样的莲花灯、梅花灯、鲤鱼灯、走马灯等。这一天潮汕人无论男女老幼，都早早用完晚餐后便上街游览赏灯，到处人山人海，欢声笑语，一派热闹欢乐的气氛。

近年来，每逢元宵佳节，潮汕三市及所属各县都举办大型花灯展，吸引了海外乡亲回乡观赏。

（三）做丁桌

在潮汕乡村，上年生过男孩的人家，元宵夜要点灯，还要在祠堂设宴请客，以庆"出丁"，俗称"做丁桌"。宴客时有两种席式，一种叫"龙船席"，即用好多只方桌联结起来，客人围在两旁吃饭，形同划龙船；另一种叫"走马席"，即无论亲朋疏厚，认识不认识的人都可以进来吃，吃完就走，主人再重新摆上饭菜，招待另一批客人的来临，接连不断。这后一种席式一般是较有钱且较慷慨的人家才会这么做。在过去，潮汕人攀比心强，爱面子，凡生了男孩的人家都十分注重办丁桌，并以办得体面为荣。即使是贫困人家，为了不失面子，也要四处借钱请客，造成负债累累，甚至是忍痛卖了哥哥，也要将所得之钱用来应付沉重的办桌费，这就是"生阿细卖阿大"这一俗语的来历。现在，潮汕人虽仍有元宵办丁桌的习俗，但多改为在自家里进行，且仅限于宴请较亲的亲戚和较好的朋友，丰俭由人，无人计较。

（四）求喜物

元宵节期间，乡村中设坛拜神。各寺庙、宗祠灯火齐明，烟雾弥漫，善男信女争先参拜，非凡热闹。神坛前所摆设的鸡、鹅、鸭、糖果、粿品、花烛、大橘（潮州柑）等祭品被视为神物。参拜的男女纷纷卜取祭品，取回家中，叫作"求喜物"。人们认为用了这些神物后，就可以让家门平安、添财添丁。卜取神物的人家，明年要照还或多还所拿的神物。于是有些人乘拥挤的机会，偷偷拿走坛前的祭品回家吃，意谓"吃兴盛"。

（五）行桥度厄

元宵节，潮汕地区大都有行桥度厄、祈求平安的习俗。这种习俗大约在明万历年间开始在潮汕流行。如今，这种习俗在潮汕一些地方还保留着。在揭阳，元宵日，男女老幼争

○行过桥

先过桥，男青年祈望日后娶贤妻；姑娘希望嫁个好夫婿，产男孩；老者祈求健康长寿；小孩则祈求长大成人。

在普宁洪阳也有"十五夜行头桥"的习俗。"头桥"指已有400多年历史的太平桥。每逢元宵夜，男女老幼共同走过太平桥，过桥时不可回头，否则"不吉利"。过桥的人还常伴有摸桥上石狮子的习俗。正在读书的小孩喜摸石狮鼻，意思是"摸狮鼻，写雅字"；未婚的小伙子希望"摸狮肚，娶雅（贤妻）"；而已怀孕的妇女则喜摸狮耳，说是"摸狮耳，生阿弟"。

（六）抢鸡肉

在揭阳南陇村，有"抢鸡肉"的有趣活动。元宵夜，人们在路边田野上搭起一个临时的简易高台，由主祭人站在高台上把一只熟鸡向台前拥挤的人群抛去。台前的人们，尤其是年满18岁以上未婚

或已婚未生子的青年，便一齐上前哄抢，以求得妻、生子。抢到鸡肉者应立即撕下一小片肉，马上把余下的再向空中抛去，让别人去抢。千万不可全部拿着走或多占，否则人们会冲他而来，推倒在地并踩上一脚，因为贪心者当年会大不吉利。这样，就形成了抛鸡—接鸡—撕鸡—再抛鸡的热闹场面。

（七）看新娘

在潮汕不少地方，结婚不久的新娘在夫家过第一个元宵节时，不论是否怀孕，都要按结婚当天的衣饰打扮如初，请宾客再上门看一回"新娘"。于是有好事的小伙子常常在深更半夜结伴上门来"搞乱"，即便这样，新郎新娘也要笑脸相迎，热情接待。这是一种婚礼的追忆仪式，好让夫妻重温新婚甜蜜日子，珍惜幸福美满的新生活。在有些乡村，所有新娘要在元宵夜由亲友相陪到祠堂祭拜神明，以祈求今年能生男孩。祭拜之后要绕堂一周观看祠堂里的灯笼，之后走出祠堂观看堂前的"皮影戏"。因此，新娘出门前必打扮得漂漂亮亮，同时十分注重自身仪态，希望能给乡人留下美好的印象。

（八）掷喜童

元宵节期间，乡村会在祠堂前广场或街头巷尾的开阔处，搭起一个彩棚，里面用泥土塑成一尊巨型的弥勒佛像。佛像光秃秃的头、肩、肚脐、大腿等部位摆设有男女"泥喜童"。所谓的"泥喜童"，是用泥做成笑容可掬、喜气洋洋的孩童塑像，大小不一。人们站在一丈多远的竹栏杆外，用铜钱瞄准弥勒佛身上的泥喜童，扔中者喜童即归其所有。而在一些较难命中的部位，如头顶、耳朵等处摆放的喜童，命中者则一赠二三不等。扔不中者铜钱即归摆弥勒佛的棚主所有。这是一项老少都喜爱的活动。据说命中"男喜童"者，今后就生男孩。因此，那些结婚不久的年轻夫妻，或者刚娶儿媳妇又急于抱孙子的爷爷们、奶奶们也积极参与此项活动。一经命中，棚主和周围的人就会向扔中者喝彩、道贺。扔中者更是喜滋滋地把"男喜童"抱回家中，认为中了头彩，有好兆头，今年定能早生贵子。

（九）荡秋千

潮汕地区荡秋千活动，以汕头市澄海区澄城港口乡、揭阳市炮台镇桃山乡、潮安县庵埠镇仙溪乡、亭厦乡等地较为有名，涌现了不少荡秋千能手，他们能在高达 10 米的秋千架上穿木屐、皮鞋表演离手倒吊、空中转身等高难度技法。

○荡秋千

与全国许多地方节日期间都有的荡秋千活动不同，潮汕有些乡村在荡秋千时出现了一些奇特的风俗。例如，揭阳市炮台镇桃山乡正月期间，男女老幼几乎天天都可荡秋千，但是元宵节那天，男人不能登上秋千棚，整个秋千活动只能由女人参与，男人只能站在一旁观看。潮州市有些乡村，元宵夜年轻夫妻要跑到村里老榕树下荡秋千，任村人往身上泼粪，说是被人泼得越多，越能在今年生男孩。

潮汕元宵节除上述主要习俗活动外，如澄海、饶平等地还要采榕树枝、竹叶回家插在门楣、灶台、禽舍，以祈人口平安、六畜兴旺；澄海、揭阳的农户要到屋外或田地里抱回灰砖或土块，放在猪栏内，称"十五夜抱大猪"，以祈饲养大猪发大财；澄海等地的少女偷偷到菜园里坐一下芥菜（大菜），说是"坐大菜，将来嫁个好夫婿"，少男则偷偷推倒厕所墙，说是将来可以娶到"雅"；普宁的客家地区新嫁娘要结伴到村边竹林里摇竹子，边摇边念："摇竹头，不用愁；摇竹尾，年底养个大乌龟（生男娃之意）"；汕头等地则举行赛大猪、赛大鸭、赛大鹅等活动及夜间抬神出游的游神活动。

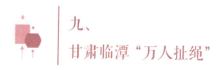

九、
甘肃临潭"万人扯绳"

在甘肃临潭县，每年元宵佳节都要举行传统的扯绳活动。"万人扯绳"成为当地元宵节期间最为壮观的一项民俗活动。

"万人扯绳"活动迄今已有600多年的历史。据文献记载：明朝洪武十二年（1379年），洮州（今临潭）十八族人叛乱，朝廷派沐英将军前去平叛。沐英军队在旧城里驻扎，就以当地称为"牵钩"（即拔河）的习俗作为军中士兵娱乐的游戏，用以增强士兵的体力。后来明朝实行"屯田戍边"政策，许多将士留在了临潭，军队里扯绳的习俗从军营里传到民间。

现在，当地群众把扯绳作为"以占年岁丰歉"的象征，反映了人们祈求丰衣足食、团结一心、安居乐业的美好愿望。

"万人扯绳"不分男女老少，不分民族，参加人数多达上万余人，场面十分壮观。活动于每年农历正月十四、十五、十六晚上举行，每晚三局，三晚九局。

届时，来自周边地区的各族群众涌向临潭县城。午后，筹办者把准备好的"绳"（主绳直径约为14厘米的钢缆绳）按传统习俗摆放在二字街中央，由民众推荐"少壮"者担任"连手"，负责每局的胜负，并与对方联结"龙头"（即绳头）。赛前，各自将绳捆扎成头连、二连、三连、连尾（俗称双飞燕）。比赛开始，参赛者一拥而上，分挽绳的两端，双方联手将木楔子串在龙头中间，开始角逐。此时圆月当空，爆竹声、哨子声、呐喊声、音乐声、观众的喝彩声融为一体。扯的绳如巨龙滚动、蛟龙出水，忽上忽下，或动或静，相争相持，

○万人拔河

167

气势为虹。

　　"万人扯绳"活动已举办多年。2001年7月，"万人扯绳"被载入世界基尼斯纪录。当时所用的扯绳，绳重8吨，"龙头"直径16.5厘米，"龙尾"直径6厘米，总长度达1808米，参与人数达15万，是"扯绳"史上最重、直径最大、长度最长、人数最多的一次比赛，盛况空前，堪称世界之最。2007年，"万人拔河（扯绳）"被列为甘肃省非物质文化遗产保护名录。

Chapter Four
Distinct Festival Customs in Different Places

Thanks to the vast territory of China, different places have preserved their distinctive customs and traditions on the Lantern Festival. The varied celebrations for the Lantern Festival in different areas have formed a dynamic picture.

1. The Lantern Festival in Taizhou City, Zhejiang Province

Compared with other places, the Lantern Festival celebration in Taizhou is unique in its origin, duration and cuisines. In Taizhou, the Lantern Festival comes on the 14th day of the first lunar month, not the 15th. Such a big difference has something to do with its unique origin.

1.1 The Story of Fang Guozhen

Fang Guozhen was born in Taizhou, in the late Yuan Dynasty. In his times, people were living too hard and many began to rise up and resist the oppression of the Yuan rulers. Fang was one of the revolution leaders. He conquered three cities Wenzhou, Taizhou and Ningbo and established his own kingdom in Linhai. However, to avoid being sneak attacked by other revolutionary armies, Fang ordered to celebrate the Lantern Festival one day ahead. In another sense, his mother believed in Buddhism, and had to abstain from eating meat and pay religious homage to temples on each 1st and 15th days of a lunar month. Fang was a filial son, so he celebrated the festival one day ahead with families merrily just to let his mother enjoy a good reunion meal.

1.2 Anti-Japan Hero: Qi Jiguang

The festival is said to be related to Qi Jiguang, an Anti-Japanese Pirates hero in the Ming Dynasty. In the age of Emperor Jiajing(1522 AD—1566 AD) Qi commanded his troops in Taizhou to celebrate the festival one day in advance just because the military secret was leaked and they had to prepare for the war the next day. When the victory was gained, the Taizhou people carry on the custom to celebrate the Lantern Festival on the 14th day just to commemorate Qi's great leadership.

1.3 The Lanterns on the 14th Night

In Taizhou, on the 14th night of the first lunar month, all the households will light up lanterns or candles. Such a tradition is said to be originated by Qi Jiguang.

In the Ming Dynasty, Japanese Pirates invaded and harassed the coastal area of China, and General Qi Jiguang was sent to fight against Japanese Pirates with the local soldiers. One day, Qi got information that the Japanese army would attack Taizhou on the 14th night of the first lunar month, thus he ordered his troops to lay ambush around the city. At the same time, Qi also called on local people to light up candles in their houses during the war. When the Japanese Pirates were defeated and fled in disorder, they found there was no place to hide because everywhere in the city was as bright as the day. Finally they were all caught alive by Qi's troops.

To honor the victory, Taizhou people have preserved the candle-lighting custom on the 14th night, and the candles and festival lanterns add colors to the lively festival celebration. Meanwhile keeping the room bright can also keep thieves away.

1.4 The Frameless Embroidery Lanterns

From the 13th or 14th day of the first lunar month, Taizhou people will hang up the festival lanterns at home for several days. The most famous local lanterns are the Frameless Embroidery Lanterns in Xianju County and Orange Lanterns in Huangyan District.

A legend said that a scholar of Xianju in the Tang Dynasty lost his way at one night and got help from a fairy who held a magic lantern to show him the right direction. When he arrived home, he and his wife made such a unique lantern to show their gratitude to the fairy. Soon this pattern of lantern became quite popular among the local people.

The lantern craftwork originated from the Tang Dynasty, so it was named "Tang Lanterns" and won the reputation of "China's Top One Lantern." The lantern has no framework. It is pasted only by papers in different sizes and shapes. Its surface is covered by an embroidery pattern paper. The whole process contains 13 steps in fine work.

1.5 The Orange Lanterns

During the age of Emperor Jianyan in the Southern Song Dynasty (1127 AD—1130 AD), Jin people from the north made inroads. Prince Zhao Gou ran away from the sea road and passed by Taizhou in Zhejiang Province on the 15th day of the first lunar month. He climbed the Jin'ao Hill and happened to see lots of illuminants floating on the river. He felt surprised and asked his men to check it. Soon the report said that those objects were Orange Lanterns. Zhao Gou went to the riverside

Orange Lanterns

172

and paid for two boats of orange. After all his men ate up the orange meat, the orange peels were made into lanterns which could float on the water.

Since then, on each 15th day of the first lunar month, Huangyan people may come to the riverside and watch the orange lanterns floating.

1.6 The Mixed Rice Flour Soup

Instead of eating sweet rice balls, Taizhou people take mixed rice flour soup on the Lantern Festival. The cooking is a little time-consuming. The soup is mainly made of rice flour, added with pork, corn niblet, dried bean curd, bamboo shoots, fava beans, leaf mustard, mushroom, taro, fried beancurd puff, etc. First, chop those materials into dices, and stir-fry the mixture in the wok. Then add water until it boils. Put flour into the wok, and keep stirring until it is totally cooked. Add flavorings before the soup is finished.

The soup has a story behind it. In the early Tang Dynasty, Taizhou was often ransacked by pirates. Soldiers were mobilized to build walls to defend against those pirates. The construction began on the 14th day of the first lunar month when the pirates landed at Taizhou Bay. Soldiers sped up the defense construction when some others were sent to fight against the pirates. On that night, the rain was pouring and the wind was blowing. Seeing the soldiers tired and cold, the common people wanted to do something for them. Some people suggested taking some wine and food which might keep them warm. While some others disagreed, "They have regulations. They cannot drink wine in a war." When all people were giving their opinions, one man said, "Why not cook vegetables and rice flour in rice wine? Such a mixed thick soup is delicious and warm." All of them gave a thumb to the idea and began to prepare the materials. When buckets of delicious thick soup were eaten, soldiers were not afraid of hunger and coldness any longer, and the speed of the construction was quickened. In the face of crisis, armies and civil people worked together and built up the defending walls. To honor the victory, Taizhou people began to keep eating mixed thick soup as a custom on the Lantern Festival.

2. The Lantern Festival in South Suzhou

Rice is the main agricultural product in Daiqian Village, Shengpu Town, Wu County, Suzhou City. On the Lantern Festival, the local people don't eat sweet rice balls but a local food Grass Paste; they even don't play lanterns, instead they stamp around the fields.

2.1 Grass Pastes

People in Daiqian Village customarily eat the Grass Paste as supper on the Lantern Festival. What is the Grass Paste? The local people often dig out a pond near a river, and lay a grass bed with some manure and litter, then cover it with river mud. Likewise, put down another grass bed, manure and mud. When several layers of grass beds are finished, people seal the pond with mud. After one month's fermentation, the stuff in the pond will become good fertilizers which are called grass paste. However, this grass paste is different from what the Grass Paste they eat. The Grass Paste is a boiled mixture of rice cakes, noodles, vegetables, and shepherd's purse. It is in appearance similar to the grass paste fertilizer, so the local people give the food such a name. Before they eat the supper, they also need to sacrifice to the Kitchen God and the ancestors. The Grass Paste can be sweet or salty, full of infinite charm. The local people say that the Grass Paste is good to the growth of both people and crops.

2.2 Stamping the Fields

After the Grass Paste supper, people begin stamping the fields. When the darkness has fallen, people, with whole families together, come to their own fields, and light up straw torches to brighten the night. People run around the fields and shout, "Stamp the field corners, and we will be rewarded a good harvest. Stamp the field corners, and pigs will grow fat and strong." When one torch is burnt down, another torch is lit up. Every corner of the fields will be placed a straw torch until it is burnt down. Villagers say, "One can foretell the harvest from stamping the field corners. If the torch flame is red, it indicates a fine harvest; if it is light red and white, it means heavy rain in the next year and a poor harvest." That explains why villagers here are crazy about stamping the fields to pray for a good harvest.

After the stamping fields activity, people will take those torches back home and stamp on the base of their own houses for an auspicious sign. Then they will stamp around the pig pens and chicken and duck nests, shouting "Stamp the pig pen, and pigs grow fat and strong; stamp the duck nest, and ducks become nice and vigorous." Every family has one or two water decks in their courtyards for washing. The local people will also stamp there. It is said that by stamping the water decks, the kids will be not drowned by ghosts in the water. When all the places are stamped on, people put all the flaming torches into the stove, which means the end of the activity.

175

3. The Lantern Gifts in Northeast China

Lantern gifts are popular in Liaoyang, Haicheng, Fengcheng and eastern part of Liaoning Province, Tonghua, Lishu in Jilin Province, and Huachuan in Heilongjiang Province. On the Lantern Festival, people send lantern gifts to the graves of their ancestors to show respect and filial piety. In Heilopngjiang, people make flour lantern in a shape of bowl, so the lantern is named "Lantern Bowl". When the flour is made into the bowl shape, those "bowls" are steamed with a cotton fibre-covered reed inserted at the top, and a bowlful of oil filled inside. Those Lantern Bowls will be sent in a proper order to the spirit tablets of ancestors, the Heaven and the Earth Gods, the Kitchen God, and to warehouse, cow and horse pens, well, grinding room, doorway and crossroads.

On festivals, the flour lanterns should be sent to the graves of the ancestors. It is auspicious to arrive early at the graves. Then light up the lanterns with one's own match, definitely not others, for it is said that other people's matches cannot bring

Flour Lanterns

176

hope and brightness to one's own ancestors.

In the east and the south of Liaoning, the flour lantern gifts are now replaced by red candles. On the night of Lantern Festival, male members of each family come and burn joss paper at the graves of their ancestors in the brightness of red candles. On the way home, they need to light up a candle at every crossroad. While female members at home also light up red candles at the kitchen stove, the pig pen, well, and barn. The local people believe that lantern gifts at the graves allow the ancestors to catch lice in light; gifts at the crossroads direct the ancestors the way back home; the lanterns also symbolize blessings from the ancestors for prosperity of life.

4. The Lantern Festival in Ningdu County, Jiangxi Province

The Lantern Festival celebrations in every village of Ningdu are distinctly different from one another.

4.1 Shishang Village: New Birth Fireworks

In Shishang Village, the most spectacular celebration is New Birth Fireworks. On the 14th and 15th day of the first lunar month, households who have given birth to a boy in the previous year will set off New Birth Fireworks, and hold a Rooster Killing sacrifice. Their relatives and friends will send firecrackers to the front of ancestral hall. The baby's maternal grandpa and grandma will invite a team of suona horn and drum for entertainment. In the afternoon, the Rooster Killing sacrifice is held at the Han Emperor Temple where all the concerned households pay homage in the order of drawing lots. After the ceremony, dragon dancing team provides a performance, and then all the households will walk to the ancestral hall by the fixed route, with the accompaniment of firecrackers, gongs and drums. After 4 pm, the firecrackers were set off at the same time. The earsplitting crackers express people's delight for new born babies.

4.2 Zengfang Village: Bridge Plate Lanterns

Those villagers, who have got new born babies or newlyweds in the previous year, have to join in the parade of Bridge Plate Lanterns. Ten lantern frames are set on a 4.5-meter-long bridge plate. On each frame base, there are seats for candles. The frame is covered with white paper topped by red paper-cuts. The number of bridge plates is determined by the number of new babies in the village. Suppose in the last year, there were altogether 20 new babies in Zengfang Village, people should make 20 rows of Bridge Plate Lanterns. When the night falls, dozens of strong men carry those plate lanterns in a cruise around the village. The whole cruise team is like a fire dragon with movements and performances. The whole activity will last for several hours until the villagers are fully satisfied.

4.3 Dabu Village: Rabbit Lanterns

In Dabu Village, there is a story about the origin of the Rabbit Lanterns. In the reign of Emperor Wanli of the Ming Dynasty, a businessman Luo from Dabu was fascinated with the handicrafts of Rabbit Lanterns when he was in Yangzhou. He acted as a dumb man so he got the chance to learn from a handicraftsman. In three years, he finally mastered the skill to make lanterns, and came back to Dabu to teach the villagers how to make lanterns.

The Rabbit Lantern exhibition is a big activity from the 10th day to the 15th day of the first lunar month for five thousand villagers in Dabu. Every household will make a Rabbit Lantern which in form is three rabbit heads with a mother rabbit in the middle and two baby rabbits at the two sides. The lantern frame is made of bamboo strip pasted by red, green, and white paper. A bowl of rice, which is immersed in tea-seed oil in advance, is put in the lantern. When the parade begins, the grass wick inside the bowl will be lit up.

With the accompaniment of drums, gongs, and *suona*, the parade of over a thousand people pass by households, lanes and roads, ponds and fields, and finally they arrive at the ancestral hall. Then the parade will go to some families who have new family members or other good things to celebrate. The host families have already prepared dinners to receive their neighbors. The Rabbit Lantern parade is believed to bring about good fortune and blessings to those families. All the Dabu villagers are in great joy during the festival days.

4.4 Jiangbei Village: Tower Lanterns

Tower Lantern is a distinct Hakka custom in Ningdu. A legend in Jiangbei has it that a local Bodhisattva Granny Yang is said to govern the village. Villagers have built the Gratitude Pavilion to pray for blessings from her. Once the prayer is fulfilled, people have to redeem a vow. Those big prayers have to be redeemed with a big lantern. That is said to be the origin of the Tower Lanterns. Another version says that the Tower Lantern is used to honor Han Emperors.

On the 14th night of the first lunar month, clouds of festival lanterns gather at the Gratitude Pavilion and then spread to every corner of the village. The Tower Lantern is 1.8 meters tall and 1.3 meters in perimeter. Its facade is pasted with various colored paper-cuts featured by romance stories, legends, flowers, and animals. The lanterns have more than 20 bowls of oil inside. When the parade begins, the oil will be lit up. With the thermal power of fire, the facades of the lanterns will rotate and give the audience a dynamic and animated drawing. In the parade, there are also Bodhisattva sedans and drum teams. The villagers also set off firecrackers to celebrate. In the evening, dramas are put on to add the festival atmosphere.

4.5 Jinxian: Rooster Rice Sculpture

The Rooster Rice Sculpture is a hand-made rice food. Since the ancient times, Jinxian people have maintained it as a Lantern Festival food and tribute for sacrifice from generation to generation. Such rice sculpture is really precious, because people usually use a bowl of rice and vegetarian diet as tribute in many places in Jiangxi Province. The food is mostly in the image of a rooster. Although there are many other images, such as pigs, dogs, monkeys, dragon, fish and fowl, Jinxian people still give that food a general name Rooster Rice Sculpture. There are other images of rice sculpture, Fortune Making Tree or Money Tree, a combination of cypress branch and rice ball or eggs.

In ancient times, birds were considered the solar essence, a symbol for the sun and masculinity, and a god for human proliferation. Rooster is regarded as a variant or substitute for bird, thus the image of a rooster is placed in front of spirit tablets or ancestral halls to show respect for life and ancestors. Meanwhile, roosters can announce the arrival of dawn and wake up the earth, for which they are believed as auspicious birds. On the Lantern Festival, Jinxian people keep that custom from generation to generation.

The Rooster Rice Sculpture cannot last for long, since it

may easily become dry and dark. So the local people usually begin the preparation in the afternoon on the 10th day of the first lunar month until the 12th day. Most people cook the food in the early morning of the 13th or 14th day, and the steamed rice ball is plump and smooth.

5. The Lantern Festival Customs in Taiwan

5.1 Pingxi: Sky Lanterns

In Pingxi town, the sky lanterns are an important part of the Lantern Festival celebration. Sky Lanterns have a long history in Pingxi. In recent years, the activity is much grander in scales. The number and the size of the sky lanterns are both getting bigger and bigger. Exquisite pictures are printed on the lanterns, and the holders may write down their own names onto them. Local people say that the higher the sky lantern flies, the more prosperous one's career becomes.

The sky lantern is also named Kongming Lantern. It is

Sky Lanterns in Taiwan

181

said that in the Three Kingdoms Period, Zhuge Kongming's army was encircled in Yangping by Sima Yi. Zhuge could not send out any soldier to ask for help, so he made a floating paper lantern and flew it to the sky as a messenger to his reinforcement. Seeing the signal, the relief troop immediately came to the rescue. And the lantern was later developed into Kongming Lantern.

The sky lantern tradition in Pingxi can be traced back to the period of Emperor Daoguang in the Qing Dynasty. The earliest residents in Pingxi were pioneers from Hui'an and Anxi counties in Fujian Province. According to the old in Shifen area, in the reign of Emperor Daoguang, Shifen area was often harassed by bandits. Villagers had to escape into the mountain. After the bandits left, those who stayed in the village set off sky lanterns as a signal that it was safe to go back home. Since it was just the 15th day of the first lunar month when the villagers came back home, the local people began to celebrate the day by flying sky lanterns to declare peace. So the lanterns are also named Prayers Lanterns or Peace Lanterns. Now, the sky lantern has become an auspicious and grand meeting in Pingxi which attracts many tourists.

5.2 Yanshui: Honeycomb Firecrackers

A saying has it that Taiwan has "sky lanterns in the north, and honeycomb firecrackers in the south". The honeycomb firecrackers refer to a most famous custom on the Lantern Festival night in Yanshui Town of Tainan County.

This custom can be traced back to the Qing Dynasty. In the summer of 1885 (the 11th year of the Emperor Guangxu), a heavy pestilence struck Yanshui and over a thousand of villagers died. Villagers could do nothing but to pray to the gods.

Since the 13th day of the first lunar month was the birthday of the Saintly Emperor Guanyu, the villagers decided to hold a ceremony to invite Guanyu to drive away the evil. They also designed the honeycomb firecrackers to frighten the plague. The divine sedan of Guanyu set off at Wu Temple, and circled around the village for a blessing. Everywhere the sedan arrived was filled with fireworks and crackers. After three-day cleansing of sulphur and gunpowder, the plague was finally driven out. Since then, the people began the three-day honeycomb firecrackers celebrations for the Lantern Festival with an honor to the Saintly Emperor Guanyu.

There is another version of the story. When the villagers prayed to gods, the Saintly Emperor Guanyu decreed to vanquish the devil for the villages. On the festival night, General Zhou Cang was designated as the pioneer, and the divine sedan of Guanyu brought up the rear with the disciples in the villages following behind. On the way they continuously set off firecrackers until the daybreak. Magically enough, the plague disappeared. Since then the fireworks display had gradually become a grand fair.

Many local people believe that the more honeycomb firecrackers the more peaceful and smoother time in the next year. Although it costs much to set off crackers, people still think it worth keeping the custom to pray for good harvest and health. Now this local custom has made Yanshui a famous tourist destination in Taiwan.

To Yanshui, the Lantern Festival is really a bee-like crazy night. Visitors from all directions come to observe the fair. If you want to enjoy the honeycomb crackers show, you have to wear complete safety equipment: a safety helmet, a mask,

183

gloves, a long-sleeved overcoat, even a rubber band to fasten the trouser legs. All is used to prevent crackers from hurting the audience. At night, thousands of crackers swarm out like a group of bees. The exploded fireworks on the night sky add joy and vigor to the peaceful town. Even those people being hit by crackers are not upset at all, because it is believed to be a blessing. The local people believe that the more and the bigger honeycomb firecrackers they have, the more prosperous their business is.

5.3 Taidong: Lord Handan and Firecrackers

Taidong, in the southeast of Taiwan, has the least population among all the counties in the island, but it is also famous for another custom "Firecrackers Towards Lord Handan." The Lord Handan has many ways of writing due to the misinformation among people in the long history. Many folklorists believe that Handan originates from Xuantan due to the mispronunciation, because there was a similar custom "Welcoming the Lord Xuantan" in the early festival celebrations in Taiwan.

There are three stories about the origin of Lord Handan. The first one says Handan is actually Zhao Gongming, the Marshal Xuantan of the Kingdom of Lu, in the *Romance of the Investiture of the Gods,* who died in his fight against Zhou troops. After accomplishing his perfection in charity and piety, he was bestowed the God of Fortune, with other names like "Silver Master", "Martial god of Fortune." The second story described Handan as a local tyrant who oppressed the weak common people. One day he was revealed by the Buddha, and greatly discerned his past sins. He stood on a bridge and asked the villagers to throw firecrackers to him until death. The third

Firecrackers Towards Lord Handan

version said the villagers could not bear the bully Handan, made him drunk in a fete, and blasted him to death. Of the three versions, the first has close connection with the folklore.

In Taidong and some other places, Lord Handan is believed to visit the places with other gods on the 15th and 16th day of the first lunar month. People say that Lord Handan is afraid of the cold, thus people prepare firecrackers to drive away the cold for him. On the other hand, he is a military officer and is believed not to fear water and fire. So to throw firecrackers means to pray for fortune. In Taidong, Hualian, Zhunan and Yanshui, crackers also mean prosperity. In the celebration, one topless person is dressed as Lord Handan in a red hat scarf, his face painted, and standing on a cane chair different from the divine sedan for god statues. On the way of the parade, the "Lord Handan" only holds a huge banyan leaf to protect himself while the audiences vigorously throw firecrackers to him. The deafening crackers fly around the "lord", which looks dangerous and thrilling to the audience, but the "lord" does not change his facial expressions. The more crackers they throw, the more good luck in making money.

Many places in Taiwan observe the Handan tradition, such as Taidong, Hualian, Yuli, Beigang, and Yilan, Zhunan. But the real-person Lord Handan can only be found in Taidong.

5.4 Penghu: Praying for Turtles

Praying-for-turtle is a quite distinct local cultural activity for the Lantern Festival in Penghu as well as a traditional custom in Taiwan. A Turtle is a miraculous animal in the world. The turtles of 1,000 years old begin to grow hairs; a 5,000-year-old one is called a divine turtle; a turtle of 10,000 years old is named a spiritualized turtle. On the Lantern Festival, all the temples in Taiwan will hold the praying-for-turtle activities. The grandest one is in Matsu Temple at Penghu.

Praying for turtle just means to pray to gods for a turtle

Praying for Turtles

gift. Such a tradition has a long history. In the past, the prayers were just for giving birth to babies. *Penghu Provincial Record* by Lin Hao in the Qing Dynasty mentioned, as quoted from *A General Record of Penghu,* that "All the temples are decorated with festival lanterns to attract visitors. In the temples, flowers and flour figures are prepared. Those who pray for children will kowtow to the gods, and get a flower or flour turtle back home to enshrine it. If they finally get a baby, they have to reward with double flowers or flour turtles." In the evolution of over a hundred years, the tradition has become not only praying for babies, but blessing for peace, health and fortune. Since 70% Penghu people are immigrants from Quanzhou where the turtle prayer custom originates, this tradition has remained in Penghu until now.

At the beginning, the turtle gift was a real turtle. Later out of environmental and animal protection, it was replaced by rice turtle. The turtle-shaped gifts were made of flour and were offered to disciples in need. With the grant of gods, the turtle gifts could be taken home to pray for peace or children. Customarily the process is very easy. Anyone who has the need can move on to any temple and pick up one small turtle gift, then burn three sticks of incense, pray to gods, practice planchette for gods' permission. Then one can insert incense in the turtle back to show his belonging. After registering, the turtle gift can be invited home for worship. It can be eaten three days later. On the next Lantern Festival, that family had only to send a bigger rice or flour turtle back to the temple. In Penghu, the interesting part of the tradition is that people who have got a turtle gift should not talk to anyone on the way home, or it is said the prayer will break halfway. The turtle will be worshiped for three days. If it is a big turtle, one has to carry it with the accompaniment of gongs and drums; at home the turtle has to be worshiped by people, and incense burning cannot stop. After the ceremony, the big turtle can be divided and sent to friends to eat for a peaceful blessing. However, the turtle head should be kept for oneself. On the next Lantern festival, people to redeem vows will order proper amount of sacrifices and send them to the temple. If the return gift is a big turtle, gongs and drums, firecrackers and a series of kowtow are needed. If one has got a prosperous business or a baby, one has to prepare a heavier rice turtle. Turtle is a symbol of longevity and a divine gift. People love it very much. So it becomes a very interesting celebration activity for the Lantern Festival.

On each Lantern Festival, residents in Penghu Islands will pray for turtle at temples while the festival lanterns are raised up at every household, and over a thousand of turtles in varied forms are offered at all temples. To attract disciples, each temple tries its best to design exclusive turtles in material or size. Meanwhile, some other activities are added into the festival celebration, such as a parade, sedans of god statues, folklore performance teams, and folk music bands.

In the past, a rice turtle was usually made of 5 to 10 kilograms of rice. Nowadays, with the improvement of people's living standard, the turtle has become bigger and bigger, and a 500-kilogram rice turtle can be found easily. Besides, the materials of turtle are also growing diversified, such as flour, meat, sticky rice, chocolate, noodle, glutinous rice cake, brown sugar, cake, jelly, rice, and candy. Now some new distinguishing types are developed, such as money turtles, gods-blessed rice super turtles, and gold turtles.

At present, the activity of praying for turtles is mainly held in some big temples like Matsu Temple, Three Saints Hall, Temple of Four Faced Buddha, Polaris Temple, Dragon Virtue Temple, and King Wen Temple. Every year, many people take part in the prayer activity. Some families even send out several candidates to compete for the turtle.

5.5 Yeliu: Harbor Cleansing

In the Bao'an Temple of Yeliu Village, Wanli Town, and Taipei City, a unique custom is kept on each Lantern Festival. And there is a legend behind it. Chen Yuanguang, a great governor and officer in the Tang Dynasty, was famous for his talents and contributions to the development of Fujian Province. After his death, he became a god in the heaven. One day, he inspired a medium boy (a profession similar to the spirit medium in the west, a medium between human and gods or ghosts) to tell the villagers that he would cleanse his spirit at the harbor on the Lantern Festival. Since then, on every Lantern Festival, all the gods worshiped in the Bao'an Temple will be invited by the villagers to the harbor to cleanse the common people.

On the festival, local people will prepare sacrifices in advance. First of all, the local gods' statues are invited to the sedan, and then four strong men carry the sedan and walk around the village until they arrive at the harbor where they will dive into the shallow sea together with the sedan to receive "spirit cleansing." The men will swim to the opposite shore and hold a fire ceremony for blessings and a good harvest. A Taoist will first pray to gods for a peaceful and smooth fire ceremony. Then wave a grass-mat around fire, and add rice and salt into the fire. The four strong men run back and forth in the fire with prayers in mouth. Soon, as instructed by the Taoist, the sedan begins to cross the fire. Those disciples who have diseases or prayers to gods will follow after the sedan with bare feet. It is said that the fire ceremony will cleanse the evil pollution to the gods' statues and they will resume their super power to bless the local people. When the fire ceremony is finished, the sedan and the disciples will cruise around lanes and streets in Yeliu to drive away evil spirits. The whole activity ends when the sedan comes back to the Bao'an Temple.

6. The Sacred Land-Fire Performance in Shanxi Province

The Sacred Land-Fire Performance is a traditional folk art in the Central Plain in China, which is a collective name for performances on sacrifices and festivals, such as stilts walking, boat dance, lion dance, dragon dance, yangko dance. Land means the Land God in the ancient times, and Fire refers to the Fire God. The Land-Fire Performance reflects ancient people's worship to land and fire.

A legend said that the Water God was so aggressive and bellicose that he broke the heavenly pillar in a rage when he was fighting with the Fire God. In no time, the sky collapsed and the earth cracked. Everywhere is in great flood. Thanks to Goddess Nvwa, the sky was repaired in time. Goulong a son of the Water God, was sorry for his father's mistake, and began to fill and level up all the rips on the land. Yellow Emperor, the ruler in the legend, appreciated his behaviors and appointed him to manage the land affairs in the world. Since then Goulong became the Land God who receives worship from the common people.

6.1 Jinzhong City: The Land-Fire Performance

In Jinzhong, there is a proverb that "If you want to live a happy life, you cannot miss the three activities: fair, drama, and Land-Fire Performance". The Land-Fire Performance in Jinzhong lasts from the 1st day to the 15th day of the first lunar month, and arrives at its climax on the Lantern Festival with the grandest lantern shows, songs and dances. According to the types of performance, there are gong-drum, yangko dance, carriage-boat-sedan dance, lantern shows, mock-animals, mock-gods or mock-ghosts performances. The gong-drum performance is featured by strong rhythm and rough decoration; the yangko emphasizes singing or dancing; the carriage-boat-sedan performance comes from people's daily means of transportation; the lantern shows combine the traditional lantern design and local culture; the mock animal or ghosts performances illustrate the conflicts between human and nature in the ancient times and people's superstition and

The Sacred Land-Fire Festival

191

reverence towards evil ghosts.

6.2 Zuoquan County: Fire Plate

In Zuoquan, "fire plate" is undoubtedly the most spectacular activity on the Lantern Festival night. The fire plate actually is a coal pile in front of houses or shops. The tower-shaped coal pile is filled with firewood. The burning coal is like a flying dragon up in the fire, which is an auspicious sign. People living miles away come and watch the fire pile for blessings. Some people even walk around the pile for three times to pray for family peace. The fire piles are one to three meters tall. In the light of the fire, performances with local characteristics are put on: songs, dances, martial arts and so on. People say, "The fire performance can bring good luck next year. It is a great joy to appreciate traditional performances beside the warm fire plate." In the past, the fire plate was used only by businessmen to attract customers, and the performers would receive cigarettes and wines in a payment for their efforts. Now, the fire plate performance has been a mass celebration in Zuoquan.

6.3 Pingyao City: The Lantern Festival Customs

In the ancient city of Pingyao, some local celebrations have been maintained on the Lantern Festival, such as the Baby-Praying Temple Fair, High Stilts Dance, and Yellow River Maze.

In the Baby-Praying Temple, a goddess of birth has been enshrined. Villagers around the temple will take turns to be on duty in the temple. On the 13th day of the first lunar month, people on duty are supposed to open the temple gate, clean up the temple and raise up red lanterns. Later they will collect money from each household to buy some offerings, such as clay babies, red dates, peanuts, walnuts, and dried persimmons. On the morning of the 15th day, the mothers-in-law of the villages will come to the temple carrying all the offerings they can prepare to pray for the birth of their future grandchildren. They will burn incense, kowtow, make wishes, and invite a clay baby back home. More importantly, they will never forget to take away some red dates and peanuts from the temple, in the hope of getting a baby as soon as possible. In some other villages, the clay baby is not invited by mothers-in-law, but by a festival parade on the evening. There are two purposes by doing so: to pursue a shared joy and to have the house-bound bride known to the neighborhood.

High Stilts Dance in Youjia Village is very famous. Its stilts dancing team is often invited to perform in other villages during the 14th and 16th day of the month. The whole performance is not only grand in scale, but also colorful and amusing in style. A cymbals band comes first, then come 30-

The Sacred Land-Fire Performance

193

odd stilts performers. With the accompaniment of cymbals, the stilts team offers continuous shows along the streets. Their exaggerated movements have inspired bursts of laughter. In the past, the team would first choose to perform in rich families; the most breathtaking movement was to jump across a long wooden desk one by one, and as a reward, the house owners would provide them with cigarettes or pocket money.

In Daobei Village, 10 kilometers north of Pingyao, the Yellow River Maze has been the most splendid celebration on the Lantern Festival. On an open ground of a football-court size, a 10,000-square-meter maze is built by villagers with sorghum stalks. The maze is over one meter tall, decorated with lanterns at an interval of 1—2 meters. The maze has many entrances, but only one leading to the exit; even the right entrance may also mislead to several paths. The maze is named "Yellow River", symbolizing its zigzag course. The maze journey is usually made on the 16th day of the first lunar month. The local people hope that the maze journey could take all the diseases away in the next year.

Tips for Tourism

The ancient city of Pingyao, Shanxi Province

Pingyao, located in the central area of Shanxi, was the best preserved ancient town in China. It is named the Town of Turtle and it well maintains the main buildings in the Ming and Qing Dynasties. The street, lanes are planned according to the traditional concept of eight trigrams. There are altogether 300 ancient buildings and sites, nearly 4,000 complete civilian houses. The streets, lanes and shops are in the original form, so the town is regarded as a living sample for cities of ancient China. It reveals a splendid and complete scroll of China's development in culture, society, economy and religions.

The walls of Pingyao were firstly built in the Ming Dynasty to defend against the north tribes. In 1370, the town was further reinforced and expanded with bricks. In the following years, it was repaired over ten times, and more towers and platforms were added. In 1703, four great gate towers were built. The walls of 6,163 meters long and 12 meters tall have divided Pingyao into two different worlds: one is traditional and the other is quite modern.

Routes: Take train from Taiyuan to Pingyao Railway Station, and then arrive in the ancient town of Pingyao by bus or taxi or on foot. Or, take coach from Taiyuan Jiannan Coach Station to Pingyao Coach Station, and then you may go to the ancient town on foot.

Ticket Price: 130 RMB for all the scenic spots

Famous Spots: Street of the Ming and Qing Dynasties, Pingyao Yamen Museum

Suggested Length of Tourism: 1—2 days

Best seasons for tourism: All year round

7. The Lantern Festival Customs in Shandong Province

7.1 Temple Fair

In Shandong, the temple fair is a popular activity during the Lantern Festival. The most famous one is the temple fair in the Penglai Pavilion.

Penglai is the starting point of the Eight Immortals Crossing the Sea in Chinese fairy tale. It is believed to be a holy place for the immortals. The temple fair here has a long history of over a hundred years. It is believed that the 16th day of the first lunar month is the birthday of Goddess of the Sea, so Penglai people attend the temple fair on that day.

Now, the annual temple fair has become a grand traditional folklore in Penglai. Every year, thousands of people from all over the country come to burn incense and pray to Buddha. In the meantime, operas and yangko dance are put on at the Penglai Pavilion and the square; delicious local specialties are available. And the whole city is full of people and joy. On the 13th and 14th day of the month, the fishermen have their own Fishing Lamp Festival; they sacrifice lanterns and tributes to the Dragon King Temple in the Penglai Pavilion to pray for blessings, peace and good harvest in the new year's fishing.

Tips for Tourism

The Penglai Pavilion

Facing South Korea and Japan across the sea, Penglai is at the northernmost part of Shandong Peninsula, near Bohai Sea and Yellow Sea, 66 nautical miles to the south of Liaodong Peninsula. With a total coast line of 86 kilometers, Penglai covers an area of 1,200 square kilometers. Thanks to its unique location, Penglai, or the fairyland, has always been famous for its beautiful scenery and hazy mirage. As a historical city in Shandong, Penglai boasts over 100 historic places of interest. The Penglai Pavilion and the Penglai Waterside City are both listed into the key cultural relic sites under national protection. Specifically, Penglai Pavilion is composed of a group of ancient buildings covering an area of 32,800 square kilometers with a floor space of 18,960 square kilometers, so it has been renowned as one of the four great pavilions in China. The main pavilion at the top of hill looks like a fairy palace, overlooking the other buildings among the trees.

Routes: Take taxi at the Yantai Laishan Airport to Yantao Coach Station, and then take tourism express bus to Penglai Coach Station. Walk for another 5 minutes to the west and you will arrive at the pavilion.

Ticket Price: 140 RMB for all the scenic sparts

Best seasons for tourism: July to September

7.2 Lantern Fair

Lantern fair is also an unmissable part in the Lantern Festival celebration of Shandong. In the city of Jinan, a province-level festival lantern fair will be held at the Spouting Spring. The fair is attractive and grand in some other places such as the Dai Temple Fair in Tai'an, Lantern Riddle Fair in Yantai Mount, Folk Art Lantern Fair at Kuisheng Park in Zibo, Yellow River Estuary Lantern Fair in Dongying, Lion Tower Lantern Fair at Yanggu in Liaocheng, Fireworks Lantern Fair in Rizhao and Laiwu Lantern Fair.

The festival lanterns can be classified into two types: static lanterns and dynamic lanterns. The static ones include wall lanterns, standing lanterns, and ceiling lanterns, mostly for

Admiring the Festival Lantern

197

interior decoration; the dynamic ones are for various exterior situations, and the commonest dynamic lantern is one with a long supporting pole that can be used when walking along the streets. A Cat Lantern is much popular among kids in Huai County. The Cat Lantern actually is not in the shape of a cat, but a Kylin (Chinese unicorn). It is made of iron wire, covered with rough silk, and painted with colors. The head, the body and the tail of the lantern are interconnected by iron wire. When it is raised up, the lantern may automatically move its head and tail, much vivid and lively. Another common dynamic lantern is Dragon Lantern of various styles. The Dragon Lantern usually contains 10 to 30 body sections. Not more than three colors are used to demonstrate its brightness and beauty: the scales on the dragon body are painted in blue, the belly, the fire flames, whiskers, and lips in pink or bright red, and other parts in black, or gold or white. The Dragon Lantern is usually accompanied with another Fire Pearl Lantern or Spider Lantern. Besides, there are other dancing lanterns such as Lion Lanterns, Boat Lanterns, Birds and Animal Lanterns. Waist Lantern actually has two sections and can be fastened at two sides of the waist. Another life-size Donkey Lantern is also tied to a dancer. When the dance begins, the dancers will hide their own legs behind the lanterns to the effect that the dancers are riding on the donkeys. Dancers usually dress themselves up as women, and move their steps forward and backward. What an amusing and funny performance! Meanwhile, kids also have their exclusive lanterns: the Butterfly Lanterns and the Goldfish Lanterns.

The local culture in Shandong gives different names and connotations to all the festival lanterns.

Snow Flower Lanterns of Cao County. This type of lantern uses sorghum stalks as the framework, and white paper as the covering on the four sides. The engraved patterns on the paper in the light of candle show brilliance and uniqueness of the lantern. Recently, new structures of the type have appeared, such as Archway Lanterns, Pavilion Lanterns, Carriage Lanterns, Furniture Lanterns, etc.

Festival Flour Lanterns of Dongming County. In the countryside of Dongming County, a flour lantern has been much popular by its appealing form and taste. It is mainly made of glutinous broom corn. First make dough with the steamed corn flour, then mould the dough with hands or scissors or bamboo tube, and finally add mung beans or black soya beans as the eyes of the animal-shaped dough. The commonest lanterns are Twelve chinese Zodiac Signs Lanterns. Each flour lantern is equipped with a bowl-shaped slot with sesame oil and cotton wick. When the lantern is lit up, it becomes glittering and sparkling. The lantern patterns are usually auspicious birds and beasts, and the placement also has strict rules. Hedgehog Lantern should be placed on a grain bin to keep mice away; Fish Lantern in the pots and cookers implies a rich life; Cattle-Horse Lantern at the shed symbolizes the thriving domestic animals. After the Lantern Festival when the lantern oil is burned out, people make those flour lanterns back to dough, and ferment it in a big container for the cooking of festival cakes.

River Lanterns of Shan County. On the 7th and 15th nights of the first lunar month, people in Shan County will float river lanterns. There are two types of river lanterns: one for hanging up on a boat or ship, the other for floating on the river with a wooden or bamboo plate at the bottom. The river lanterns there are mostly made of reeds and bamboo strips, decorated with color paper, in different structures of peony, lotus, silk ball, vase, etc. The lantern has a candle or oil wick inside. When a string of river lanterns are swinging on the water, the night becomes colorful and twinkling.

Old Ox Lanterns of Weifang City. Weifang festival lanterns enjoy a good reputation of diversity and delicacy, and the most famous one is the Old Ox Lantern. When the Lantern Festival comes around the corners, the local people begin to make an Old Ox Lantern of 7 or 8 meters long at the Beach of Bailang River. After it is finished and lit up, many people come to appreciate and touch the lantern. The folk song has it that one will not get eye disease after touching the Old Ox Lantern. In addition, all families may produce calf lanterns for joy.

7.3 The Storytelling Fair at Huji Town

The Huji Storytelling Fair, lasting from the Spring Festival to the Lantern Festival, is a grand meeting in Huimin County. It has a long history of over 700 years, starting from the Yuan Dynasty, and arriving at its climax in the early years of Qing Dynasty. The fair originated from a folk art performing competition, and later developed into an interactive folk art custom. Huji is the biggest commercial town for miles around.

On the 12th day of the first lunar month, Huji embraces its first fair in a new year. People living nearby swarm into Huji and purchase the festival products. Folk storytellers from all directions also take the opportunity to provide performances. In no time, Huji has become an exciting place for storytelling. The fair is formed.

The fair can be classified into three stages: the prelude, the main festival, and the epilogue.

Before the 11th day of the month, storytellers from Shandong and other provinces carry their instruments and luggage to Huji. They give storytelling performances on their halfway, and that is called "prelude."

On the morning of the 12th day, all storytellers finally arrive at Huji. They arrange their stall and put up their banners. The Storytelling Fair formally begins. The main festival lasts from the 12th to the 16th day of the month, including many traditional art performances like Dragon Lanterns, Yangko Dance, high stilts, variety shows and martial arts. This period is also a peak time of wages for those performers. The fair also witnesses varied types of folk art: West River Bass Drum, Board Drum, Bamboo Clappers, Storytelling, Bohai Bass Drum, Shangdong Clappers, Shandong Musical Clappers, and Bamboo Percussion. The villagers around Huji are in favor of storytelling and send out "experts" to select good programs and

The performance on the storytelling Fair at Huji Town

201

storytellers who will be invited to perform in their villages. The villagers will pay for that. Since the 12th night of the month, the storytelling will continue for several days and nights at every village. If the villagers urge them to stay, they will continue their performances, and if not, they will go to the fair on the 17th day.

The epilogue of the fair is during the 17th and 21st day of the month. The fair is totally finished only when the epilogue has passed.

During the fair, all the folk art performers will send New Year greetings to each other, exchange thoughts and skills, and take disciples or teachers. After the fair, they go back to their journey of performances. And they will get together in Huji at the same time next year.

8. The Lantern Festival Customs in Chaoshan Area of Guangdong Province

The Lantern Festival in Chaoshan area has some interesting and unique customs.

8.1 The New Birth Lantern

In Chaoshan dialect, "Deng" (lantern) sounds similar to "Ding" (family member), so "to light up a lantern" means "to add a new family member". People in Chaoshan hang up lanterns during the 11th and 18th day of the first lunar month. On the Lantern Festival, people carry lanterns and joss paper to the nearby temple, light up their lanterns in the temple, take them back at the home shrine or bedsides. Such a lantern is named New Birth Lantern.

If having given birth to a boy in the past year, one family has to hang a pair of red lanterns on the 13th day of the month.

A red paper with the boy's name is pasted on the lantern at the ancestral hall, standing for a new family member. The baby will also be taken to the hall and receive neighbors' congratulations in the candlelight of the red lanterns.

During these days, some other folk activities are also held, such as lantern fair, bride show, and birth party.

8.2 The Lantern Fair

The lantern fair in Chaoshan has a long history. One may find origins in the Teochew Opera *Romance of Lychee and Mirror* of the Ming Dynasty version.

On a Lantern Festival, Chen San encountered Huang Wuniang in Chaozhou's lantern fair on his way to Quanzhou. They fell in love with each other at the first sight and finally got married after a long story. The 6th scene of the opera was set at a lantern fair in Chaozhou: "On the Lantern Festival night, all the people, well dressed, come out to enjoy the lantern fair. The fair is as splendid as the legendary turtle hill. The pictures on them bring life to the lanterns..." The fair got more prosperous in the Qing Dynasty when the Chaozhou people held a 3-day lantern fair and competition in a temple fair. With years passed, the Chaozhou lantern fair had become much popular and famous in China, and the handicrafts of lantern panel had reached a high level by the late Qing Dynasty.

Now, the lantern parade, sponsored by civil organizations and business shops, begins with a torch and a dragon lantern. Then follows the small gongs and drums, and festival lanterns, and finishes with a five-color phoenix. Different from Beijing Palace Lanterns, Shanghai's Dragon Lanterns and Guangzhou's Horse-Galloping Lanterns, Chaozhou Lanterns have varied structures and distinct styles such as silk lanterns, and real settings. The theme of lanterns may cover flowers and fruits, fish and insects, birds and beasts, operas or legends. All kinds of lanterns such as Lotus Lantern, Plum Blossom Lanterns, Carp Lanterns, and Horse-Galloping Lanterns, are decorated along streets and lanes, at shops and houses, in ancestral halls and rooms. After dinner time, women and men, the young and the old, all pour into streets to enjoy the lantern fair. The whole city is filled with people, laughter and joy.

In recent years, on each Lantern Festival, all the cities and counties in Chaoshan area will hold large-scale festival lantern shows which attract many overseas Chaoshan people to come back for a visit.

8.3 The Birth Party

In the countryside of Chaoshan, people who have given birth to a boy in the past year shall light up lanterns on the festival night, and hold a banquet or "birth party" at the ancestral hall to celebrate the new birth. The banquet can be in either of the two ways. The first is Dragon Boat Banquet: many square tables are arranged together in a form of dragon boat. The second is Horse Galloping Banquet that is continuously served to any visitors even strangers. The wealthy and generous families prefer to the second one. Traditionally, Chaoshan people paid great attention to the scale of birth party out of comparison and vanity, thus they even contracted debts to hold the banquet. A local saying has it that one can do nothing but sell the elder child to hold a birth banquet for the little baby. Although it is an exaggeration, but a vivid description of people's dilemma. Now, the custom is mainly held at home and is confined to relatives and close friends. The scale and expenditure are no more a big concern.

8.4 Inviting Auspicious Oblation

Many villages will set up altars to worship gods. All temples and ancestral halls are receiving prayers of believers in a mist of incense and lantern light. In the front of altars, the sacrificial offerings are regarded as auspicious oblation, such as rooster, goose, duck, candies, cakes, candles, and Chaozhou oranges. Believers invite home that ablation in a good hope of peace, fortune and new birth. Those who take auspicious oblation away have to return the same or more items. So somebody even takes those offerings for meals, seeking for family prosperity.

8.5 Bridge Crossing for Good Luck

In Chaoshan, people cross bridges to pray for good luck and peace on the Lantern Festival. This tradition began to prevail in the reign of Emperor Wanli of Ming Dynasty. Now the tradition has still been remained in some places in Chaoshan area. In Jieyang, on the Lantern Festival, men and women, the young and the old, are competing to cross the bridges. Young lads pray to marry a good wife; ladies wish to marry a good husband and give birth to a boy; the old bless for health and longevity; the kids hope to grow up soon.

In Hongyang Town of Puning City, people also keep the bridge-crossing custom at the night of Lantern Festival. The bridge here refers to the Peace Bridge of more than 400 years old. It is said that one should not look back when he or she is going across the bridge, or it will bring bad luck. People also touch the stone lions along the bridge. The children of school age love to touch the nose of the lions, which stands for good handwriting; unmarried lads touch the belly, which symbolizes a good wife; the pregnant women like to touch the ears, which means a blessing for giving birth to a boy.

8.6 A Rush for Chicken Meat

In Nanlong Village of Jieyang City, a funny custom is being put on. On the Lantern Festival night, a temporary platform is set up near the fields. The host on the platform tosses a cooked chicken to the crowd who are mainly young men above 18 years old without marriage or children yet. The crowd rush forward to catch the chicken meat, which means to pray for a good wife or a healthy baby. People who have caught the chicken should tear one slice of the meat and throw the rest back to the sky. If he takes possession of extra or all meat, the crowd shall rush towards him, push him down and step on him, because a greedy man should receive bad luck in the new year. Just in this way, people celebrate the festival by tossing, catching, splitting and tossing again the chicken meat.

8.7 The Bride Show

In many places in Chaoshan, the new brides have to wear the wedding dress again on their first Lantern Festival at the bridegroom's home, and invite all the guests to see the bride show. Some meddlesome lads often choose midnight to visit the new couple for this show. Even so, the bride and bridegroom have to welcome them with smiles, and hospitability. This is a recollection of their wedding ceremony which reminds the couple to value the happy memory. In some villages, on the festival night, all the brides should go to the ancestral halls to pray for giving birth to a boy in the new year. After that, they have to travel around the hall and watch the lanterns, and then they walk out the hall to appreciate the leather-silhouette show at the front of the hall. For these reasons, the brides need to pay much attention to their own appearance and manners, hoping to leave a good impression on the audience.

8.8 Tossing Clay Babies

During the Lantern Festival, a color canopy is set up at the open area near the ancestral hall or a lane. A giant clay Buddha statue is arranged inside the canopy, and clay babies of different sizes are placed at the head, shoulder, navel, or legs of the statue. People, standing outside a fence three meters away, toss copper cash towards the clay babies. If it is shot, the clay baby can be taken home. If not, the copper money will not be returned. Some clay babies are sitting at a hard-to-catch position such as the head-top and ears, and if they can be shot correctly, the shooter will be rewarded with another one or two clay babies. This is a popular activity among the young and the old. It is said that if one can get back a clay boy, one will get a real boy in life, so those new couples and those grandmas and grandpas who wish for a boy are active in this program. All the audience will congratulate the ones who get the clay boy. And the clay boy is seen as a good omen for the future birth and fortune.

8.9 The Swing Games

The swing is much popular among some towns in Chaoshan area, such as Gangkou Town of Shantou City, Taoshan Town of Jieynag City, Xianxi Town and Tingxia Town of Chao'an Gounty. Many first-class swing players are constantly emerging. They can perform some difficult movements in the air such as dangling upside down, quick turning around.

Different from the swing activities in other places, Chaoshan swings have some particular customs. In Taoshan Town of Jieyang, on the 15th day of the first lunar month, only women have access to the swings, while men could only watch at the side. In some villages of Chaozhou, young couples play the swings at the festival night while other villagers may throw dung onto their clothes; the more dung they get, the more possibility they will give birth to a boy in the following year.

On the Lantern Festival, In Chenghai and Raoping area, people pick up banyan and bamboo leaves and insert them at the doorhead, the kitchen, and the shed to pray for peace and prosperity. In Chenghai and Jieyang, farmers may take home bricks or soil blocks and put them inside the pigsties, for a blessing of fortune. In Chenghai and some other places, girls slide into a vegetable garden and sit on heliotrope which is believed a sign for marrying a good husband; while young men may sneak and push down the toilet wall, which means to marry a good wife. In the Hakkas area of Puning, the brides will go to the bamboo forest and shake the bamboos, reading, "Shaking the bamboo top, I will not worry about life; shaking the bamboo roots, I may give birth to a boy." In Shantou, domestic animal competitions are held in the day, and gods' statues parade is arranged at night.

9. The Grand Tug-of-War in Lintan County, Gansu Province

On each Lantern Festival in Lintan, Gansu Province, ten thousand people are involved in a tug-of-war activity. This is the grandest custom in the local festival celebrations.

This tradition can be traced back to 600 years ago. According to documents, in 1379, the imperial court sent an army to Lintan to oppress the rebellions. The imperial army adopted tug-of-war as a way of entertainment to improve the soldiers' physical strength. Later when the Ming Dynasty asked garrison troops to open up wasteland, many officers and soldiers stayed in Lintan, so the game of tug-of-war was passed down from the army to the common people.

Now, the local people see tug-of-war as a way to foretell the harvest next year. It has demonstrated people's good desire for a rich, harmonious and peaceful life.

Ten thousand people of all ages and both sexes, regardless of ethnic groups, take part in the tug-of-war activity on the evenings of the 14th, 15th and 16th day of the first lunar month. There are usually three rounds of competition a night, and altogether nine games for the three nights.

On the evening, people rush to the town. The rope (usually a wirerope with 14-centimeter diameter) has already been placed in the middle of the street. Strong young men act as the commanders and pioneers at the middle of the rope. Before the games, each side will bundle up the ropes into several branch ropes. When the game begins, all the people rush to their positions and pull back. The moon in the night sky sees the harmony of firecrackers' blowing, whistles, slogan, music, and cheers. The rope is just like a gigantic dragon flying out of the sea, moving up and down, back and forth, in an imposing manner.

This activity has been held for many years. In July 2001, it was entitled as a Guinness Record. The rope for the record was 8 tons in weight, 1,808 meters in length, with the rope head of 16.5 centimeters in diameter, and the tail of 6 centimeters in diameter. Nearly 150, 000 people participated in it. So that game in 2001 was the grandest one in the world with the heaviest rope, the longest diameter, the longest rope, and the most participants. In 2007, the tug of war of ten thousand people was listed in the Intangible Cultural Heritage list in Gansu Province.

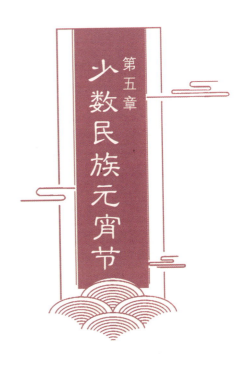

第五章 少数民族元宵节

　　受不同时期汉文化的影响，很多少数民族都将元宵节纳入了本民族的节庆礼仪中，同时添加了许多本民族文化的元素，从而使元宵节更加丰富多彩。

一、土家族元宵节习俗

在湖北恩施土家族地区，与全国各地精彩纷呈的元宵节习俗相比，乡村里的元宵节显得古朴而豪放。

（一）放路烛、耍毛狗子

正月十五晚上，村民要点亮屋内所有的灯，还要准备耍毛狗子（狐狸）和放路烛。这是十五晚上比较重要的活动。

天黑之前，村里的大人小孩都会为晚上的放灯而忙碌。当地有"三十晚上的火，十五晚上的灯"的说法。这里的灯包括三个内容，一是点亮家里所有的灯；二是放路烛，就是在自家门前的平地或路边摆放数十根点燃的蜡烛；三是搭毛狗子棚，准备用来点篝火，耍毛狗子。

元宵节前，大人小孩一起准备路烛。以前，只有松香路烛和竹筒路烛，现在出现了蜡烛。松香就是松树油干了以后结成的白色颗粒。正月十五，人们在地上一点一点地燃烧松香，然后用裹了一层棉花的小棍去搅烧化了的黑色松香油，等松香油粘在小棍上冷却后就变成了一支路烛。松香熔化时，发出"嘶嘶"的响声，散发出浓烈的香味。制作松香路烛的过程充满乐趣，同时也寄托了人们对新年美好的祝愿。

竹筒路烛，就是煤油路烛，所用的燃料是煤油。制作竹筒路烛时，人们把直径约2厘米的竹子砍成一尺来长的小竹筒。每支竹筒都留有竹节，便于装煤油，再用纸搓成灯芯，卷成圆形后塞在竹筒顶端，倒上煤油，一支路烛就做好了。

在当地，路烛的数量是有讲究的，做12支象征月月顺利；做15支代表当日正好是"过十五"。当然，还可以根据个人的喜好做20支等。路烛做好后，放在家门口平坦的地方，或场坝前、大路边，所放路烛的位置要方便河对岸人观看。当地人说，放路烛可以保佑来年吉利、顺心。

关于毛狗子，还有一个故事。据说很早以前：土家的先人们以为毛狗子聪明伶俐，就把它当作朋友请来家里做客。毛狗子在土家老乡家里吃跑喝足后还不知足，走的时候还偷了土家人的鸡。人们发现毛狗子的丑事以后，不再和它交朋友了。可毛狗子的本性难改，还是常常来偷鸡。有一年的正月十五，村里的人都出去耍狮子了，家里无人看守。毛狗子就乘机偷光了一户老乡家里的鸡。主人回来后，看到家里的鸡全不见了，很恼火，说肯定是毛狗子干的。于是召集村民，找到毛狗子住的地方，一把火烧了它的老窝。从那以后村里就六畜平安无事了，也就有了正月十五赶毛狗子的习俗。后来，人们用火和喊声来表达最朴实的愿望：驱逐野兽，保护家禽家畜兴旺。

由此赶毛狗子、烧毛狗子棚的习俗也就流传了下来。先要搭建毛狗子棚，就是全村男女老少一起出动，将捡来的干枯树枝、竹枝等搭成一人多高的棚子，一般搭在屋外空旷的地方，一来可避免火灾，二来可以让河对岸的人看到。

（二）吃年根

　　土家族在饮食上除了吃汤圆以外,最具特色的就是吃"年根"(猪尾巴)。元宵节时,各家除了准备丰盛的菜肴以外,还要准备的食物就是"年根"。大年三十会在家里吃猪头肉,正月十五则吃"年根",象征着春节的结束,也象征一年到头"有头有尾"。在当地,"年根"要从大年三十做年饭起就与猪肉一起煮熟,但是不能先吃掉,一直要保存到正月十五。到时,家里的每位成员都要吃,据说这样能把好运带给大家,而且家里的男主人要吃根部最粗的那一节。

（三）互赠十五粑

　　在湖北省长阳土家族自治县,正月十五这一天,土家人家家户户都要做十五粑。十五粑是用苞谷面做成的苞谷粑粑,香甜、个大,馅分荤素两种。正月十四,各家各户事先都准备苞谷面和各种馅。正月十五一大早,各家便开始忙着做十五粑。首先在浸泡好的苞谷

○土家族姑娘

面里包上馅，然后捏成圆形的粑粑，再放到格子里蒸。一次蒸一格，一格里放十二个粑粑，依次代表十二个月。同时在每个粑粑上用大拇指摁一个小窝，待把粑粑蒸熟后，观察每个小窝里的水分。哪个小窝水分多，预示这个月雨量充足；若水分少，预示这个月雨水少，有干旱。然后将蒸熟的十五粑拿到门外敬五谷神，祈求当年五谷丰登。敬完五谷神后，各家各户还要互赠十五粑。当地有这样的说法："十五粑送得越多越好，因为它代表着团圆友好，也预示着这一年的开局好。"

二、
苗族偷菜节

苗族偷菜节流行于贵州省黄平一带，于每年农历正月十五日举行。节日这天，姑娘们三五成群邀约在一起去偷别人家的菜，但是严禁偷本家族，也不能偷同姓朋友家的，据说偷菜与她们的婚姻大事有关。所偷的菜是白菜，数量够大家吃一顿就行。偷菜不怕被人发现，被偷的人家也不会责怪姑娘们。大家把偷来的菜集中在一起，做成白菜宴。谁吃得最多，谁就能早得意中人，谁养的蚕就最壮，蚕吐出的丝也最好最多。

偷菜节也是孩子们的节日。据说夜里有小孩子们去"偷"菜，

215

预示着今年有个好收成；吃了孩子们偷来的菜，全年不会生病生疮。所以正月十五夜也是最开心快乐的节日，孩子们吃过晚饭后就开始准备偷菜节的活动了。晚上，圆月明亮，孩子们三五成群地相约去野外菜地里偷摘新鲜的蔬菜，他们无论偷谁家菜地的蔬菜，大人们都不能去现场抓赶，只能在远处大喊"抓偷菜贼"，吓吓他们。孩子们也知道十五夜里偷菜不算贼。听到喊声，一些稍大的孩子会戏闹般地叫别人"快跑！快跑！"然后又跑去另外的地里继续"偷"。小伙伴们在月光下打闹嬉戏，唱歌玩耍，直到月亮快到中天了，才开始偷摘别人菜地里白菜苔、大蒜苗之类的蔬菜。偷菜节去偷菜只能空着手去别人的菜地摘菜，不能背篮子或者是挎着箩筐去偷，否则大人就会打人。也不能偷得太多，一人用手偷一把菜就足够了。孩子们偷好菜后带回家，然后动手把偷来的菜做好，请家人及邻居们来吃。大人们边吃边评论孩子们厨艺的好坏，孩子们则边吃边说偷菜的经过，家中洋溢着欢声笑语直到午夜。

Chapter Five

The Lantern Festival of Minority Ethnic Groups

Under the great influence of Han culture, almost all minority ethnic groups in China celebrate the Lantern Festival and add their own ethnic elements to the festival customs.

1. The Lantern Festival Customs of Tujia Ethnic Minority

In Enshi of Hubei Province, where people of the Tujia ethnic group live in concentrated communities, the Lantern Festival celebration is of primitive simplicity and boldness, compared with other places.

1.1 The Roadside Candles and the Fox Shed

On the festival night, villagers will illuminate all the lights, and prepare the roadside candles and the fox shed, two important activities for Tujia people.

Before it is dark, villagers are keeping busy for the lights at night. The lights here refer to three sources: the lamps' light at home; the candles' light at the open space or at the roadside near the house; and the campfire near a fox shed.

The roadside candles are prepared in advance. In the past, there were only colophony candles and bamboo candles, now they have wax candles. The colophony is the white granules crystallized from pine oil. When the colophony is burnt down into black oil, a cotton-covered stick is used to stir it until the oil is cooled together with the stick. Then a roadside candle is made. The colophony gives off a strong incense and a low noise in the burning. The process is full of joy and good wishes for the new year.

The bamboo candles are actually kerosene candles. The bamboo tube is two centimeters in diameter and 30 centimeters in length. Each tube has a bamboo joint for the storage of kerosene. Paper wick is filled in the top of the tube. Then a bamboo candle is finished.

There are rules on the number of roadside candles. Twelve candles symbolize the twelve smooth months in a year; Fifteen candles mean the celebration of the 15th day of the first lunar month. However one can decide the number out of one's own preference. The candles should be placed at level areas near the house, or the threshing ground, or the roadside, to be easily seen by the people opposite the river bank. The local people believe that the roadside candles may bring blessings and fortune next year.

There is a story about the fox. Long ago, the Tujia ancestors mistakenly believed a fox as a clever animal and invited it to be a guest at home. The fox ate and drank to its satisfaction, and stole a chicken when it left. People soon realized its dishonesty and stopped contacting with it. But its nature is hard to change. The fox often came and stole chickens. On a Lantern Festival, when villagers went out to play lion dance, the fox sneaked into a house and stole out all chickens. The owner was very angry about that, and called together all the villagers to find the shed of the fox and burnt it down. Since then, the village had never been troubled by the fox. But the custom of driving the fox has been remained. Later, people use fire and yelling to express their simple wishes: to protect domestic animals from beasts.

The custom of burning the fox shed are still preserved now. To start with, all the villagers will work together to set up a 2-meter-tall fox shed with dry branches and bamboos. The shed is usually arranged at an open area for two reasons: to avoid fire disaster and to have it seen by the people at the opposite river bank.

1.2 The Festival Tails

On the festival, Tujia people eat sweet balls and the Festival Tails (pig tails actually). The tail is an unmissable dish for every Tujia family on the Lantern Festival. Tujia people eat pig heads on the Spring Festival Eve, and eat pig tails on the Lantern Festival, which stands for a closure of the Spring Festival holidays and a continuity of all-year-round wealth. Of course, the pig tails are cooked together with meat on the Spring Festival Eve, but they are kept uneaten until the 15th day of the month. Each family member has to eat one, because the festival tail is believed to bring good luck, and the male host should eat the fattest section.

1.3 Exchanging Festival Cakes

In Changyang Tujia Autonomous County of Hubei Province, every Tujia family will make festival cakes on the Lantern Festival. This festival cake, sweet and big, is made of corn flour, with either meat or vegetable fillings. On the 14th day of the first lunar month, corn flour and fillings are prepared. On the morning of the Lantern Festival, the making of cakes begins. First add fillings into the corn flour, and mould them into round cakes, and then steam them in a pot. Every time 12 corn cakes are steamed, standing for 12 months of a year respectively. Meanwhile, press into a small pit on each cake with thumb. When the cakes are steamed well, watch the water level of each pit. The cake with more water in the pit indicates the month with adequate rain; the cake with less water in the pit shows the possibility of drought in this month. The steamed corn cakes will be offered to Five Cereals Gods to bless a good harvest. In addition, people also exchange festival corn cakes with their neighbors. There is a local saying, "The exchange of festival corn cakes symbolizes reunion and friendship, and shows a good start of a new year. So it is better to send more cakes to others."

2. Vegetable Stealing Day of Miao Ethnic Minority

Vegetable Stealing Day of Miao ethnic minortiy is popular among Huangping area in Guizhou Province. It is also celebrated on the 15th day of the first lunar month. On the festival, girls gather in groups to steal vegetables, neither from their own clan, nor from friends of the same surname, because that may influence their future marriages. Of course, the stealing will not be criticized or punished at all. But the stolen vegetables should be barely enough for a dinner of the group. Those girls will collect all the vegetables together and cook a vegetable dinner. According to the local belief, whoever eats the most will find her Mr. Right soon, and her silkworm will grow stronger and produce silk in best quality and in largest quantity.

The festival is also a joyful day for children. If children steal vegetables at the festival night, there will be a good harvest this year. And the vegetables stolen by children may have a miracle power to drive away diseases. Such a belief has brought a greatly

Young Miao Girl

joyful night to children. After supper on the festival, children begin to act for the night stealing.

When the moon is shining brightly in the night sky, children in groups go to fields to steal fresh vegetables. No man will actually arrest them, but only yell and frighten them afar. The children are also aware of the "rule." Hearing the yelling, some elder kids may jokingly ask other kids to run away while they themselves continue to steal in another field. Deep into the night, those young kids begin to steal cabbages or garlic sprout. There are some rules to obey: no baskets or other tools can be used in stealing, or they will receive punishment; do not steal more than enough for one meal. When they take the vegetables back home, the kids have to cook a meal by themselves and invite other family members and neighbors to enjoy it. Adults taste and comment on the dinner, while the kids share their stealing stories. The whole family is surrounded by laughter and joy until midnight.

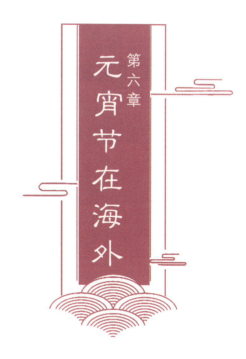

第六章

元宵节在海外

元宵节不仅在中国备受青睐，世界各地的人们同样有着过元宵节的习俗，元宵节也因此在世界其他国家生根发芽。

一、
元宵节在澳大利亚

　　澳中友好交流协会堪培拉分会每年都在柏莱格里芬湖畔举行庆祝元宵节的活动。为了准备庆祝元宵佳节，堪培拉分会组织4岁以上的孩子们参加灯笼制作学习班，让他们学习制作各种纸灯笼。分会提供各种材料，包括薄板纸、胶纸、胶水、剪刀、灯笼图样、玻璃纸、蜡烛、竹劈儿，以及有关制作灯笼的说明书。灯笼制作学习班备受欢迎，学员经常爆满。同时，学习班鼓励学员带着自己的灯笼去参加手工制作的灯笼比赛。

○澳中友好交流协会堪培拉分会举行的元宵节活动

元宵节下午，分会会员们忙着往树上挂彩灯、中国结和灯笼，准备要卖的灯笼和蜡烛，陈列供随意取阅的中国书籍。元宵节庆祝活动开始前，来自堪培拉普通社区的居民齐聚会场。节目开始时，先由主持人简单介绍元宵节的来历，接着由中国驻澳大利亚大使致辞。然后便开始精彩演出。夜幕降临，树上的灯笼和彩灯特别引人注目。最后举行提灯游行，由两只狮子领头，组成 500 名观众的游行队伍。

二、元宵节在韩国

正月十五的元宵节，韩国人称为"元夕节"。韩国没有元宵节的说法，正月十五直接就叫作"正月大望日"，意为"望满月"。

十五这天要吃五谷饭、坚果、干菜，还要喝"清耳酒"。五谷饭是混合糯米、高粱米、红小豆、黄米、黑豆等杂粮做成的饭。杂粮不易煮，最正宗的做法本来是用传统石锅来做，但随着科技的发展和人们生活节奏的加快，改用电压锅来做。虽叫"五谷"，但也没那么严格，跟中国

◎ 韩国元宵五谷饭

225

第六章 元宵节在海外

的腊八粥相似。家里的杂粮，统统混合在一起煮。正月十五吃五谷饭，据说一方面是为了在冬天补充营养，另一方面是为了寄托对新一年健康和丰收的希望。和五谷饭一起吃的还有干菜，是用前一年秋天晾干存起来的茄子、西葫芦、萝卜缨、山野菜等做成的。据说正月十五吃干菜，这年的夏天就不会中暑。同时，还要吃各式各样的坚果，如花生、核桃、松仁、栗子、银杏等，据说可以使牙齿更坚固，还能防治疔疮等皮肤病。元夕节早上喝的"清耳酒"，也叫耳明酒。据说喝过了耳明酒，就意味着全年都能听到好消息，耳朵不会得病，而且会变得更灵敏。韩国的清酒是用"纯米"酿造的，散发着扑鼻的清香，入口分外纯美。

○韩国"烧月亮屋"的祈福活动

在韩国过元宵节，还要举行各种各样的祈福活动和民俗游戏。其中有一个重要的活动叫"烧月亮屋"。在农村，全村人聚到一起，在宽敞的空地上用树干或竹子搭成圆锥形的屋架，上面盖满松枝和稻草，同时挂上写着新年愿望的纸条，这就是"月亮屋"。圆月升起之后，人们用手中的火把点燃"月亮屋"，围着火堆欢歌起舞。树干和竹子燃烧时发出"噼里啪啦"的响声据说可以驱走恶鬼。火烧得越猛烈，就预示着这一年的年景越兴旺，如果火半途熄灭，会被视作凶兆。此外，还有放风筝、拔河、踏桥等其他活动，意在驱病、除灾、祈福等。韩国江原道的春川市、三陟市、济州岛等地每年正月十五都会举行庆典活动，元宵节充满了别样的意趣。

三、
元宵节在马来西亚

　　元宵节是马来西亚华裔重大的传统节日之一，其中的"抛柑接蕉"习俗热闹浪漫、别具一格。

　　"抛柑接蕉"的习俗有一个来历。在古代，无论是大家闺秀还是普通人家女子平时很少出门，只有到了元宵节，才被家长破例允许结伴出门看灯赏玩。不少男女便借机物色心上人，擦出

○抛柑接蕉

许多爱情的火花。这个习俗传到马来西亚后，变成了"抛柑接蕉"的习俗。起初，是由祖籍福建的马来西亚未婚女子开始的，称为"抛好柑，嫁好尪（意为丈夫）"。如今，演变成一个男女青年交流结识的节日，大家热热闹闹地在元宵夜向大海、湖泊或池塘抛水果，女抛柑橘，男掷香蕉，还在水果上写上电话号码，以期觅得一段好姻缘。许多单身男女参加"抛柑接蕉"活动，希望用这个方式让自己"捞到"一个好姻缘。如今，在吉隆坡、雪兰莪州、槟城和马六甲等地，仍有这样的习俗。在吉隆坡，年轻人围坐在喷水池周围，待柑橘和香

蕉抛入水中后,男性会去捞柑,女性则去拾蕉。在霹雳州,华人社团会在怡保观音洞举办"你挂柑我采柑"的活动,年轻人用红线将自己的相片和柑橘绑好,挂在许愿树上,希望就此结识可以携手相牵的伴侣。

吉隆坡蕉赖敦拉萨镇的皇后公园,在公园喷水池进行的抛柑活动已经有12届。公园内建有一个抛柑池,方便男女青年在池内捞柑。除了抛柑,也有放水灯、祈福等活动让公众参与。八打灵的再也公园已经举办了多次抛柑活动,公众反应热烈。除了可以自行携带外,现场也售卖许愿柑、许愿球、许愿纸和一些小食品,琳琅满目。在槟城,历年元宵节抛柑活动都在旧关仔角海堤旁进行。在马六甲河,凡搭乘游船者,都可免费获得一个柑。乘客可在柑上写上愿望或祝福语,然后随着游船到河上指定地点,将柑抛进河里,祈求愿望成真。单身男女也可在柑上写下姓名与联络号码,以求姻缘。

○抛柑接蕉

多彩中国节

元宵节

四、
元宵节在日本

在日本，把正月十五称为"小正月"，这个称呼是对于元旦的大正月而来。日本的元宵节没有吃汤圆的习惯，但是早上有吃红豆粥的习俗，不过现在仅有部分农村地区得以保存。每到这天，几乎家家户户都要煮一大锅红豆粥，据说吃了可以消灾避祸。不过，元宵吃红豆粥的习俗最早也是由中国传入。

○日本灯笼

自唐代以后，在中国江南产桑蚕地区，以前正月十五煮粥祭祀的习俗逐渐演变成以糯米做成粉，包成形似蚕茧的圆子，叫作元宵或汤圆。后来，中国各地都慢慢地改变了元宵节吃赤豆粥的习俗。在日本，这个习俗被视为传统典范而固定下来，成为元宵节饱含着美好祝愿的民俗的一部分。

农历正月十五这天，日本境内的中华街都要举行闹元宵活动。横滨中华街每年都举办元宵节赏花灯活动，一些当地的华人华侨都前去观看。整条街上被装点得五彩缤纷，到处充满节日气氛。赏花灯活动在傍晚开始，同时，还会举行一些舞龙、舞狮和传统舞蹈表演。一些日本人也前来赏花灯，欣赏精彩的节目，无不被这样的节日气氛所感染。

Chapter Six
The Lantern Festival in Other Countries

The Lantern Festival is not only popular in China, but also favored by people of other different countries. Therefore, it has been deeply rooted and developed in many other countries.

1. The Lantern Festival in Australia

The Lantern Festival is celebrated every year in Canberra Branch of Australia-China Friendship Society near the Lake Burley Griffin. Before the festival celebration, the Canberra Branch will organize lantern-making classes for learners above 4 years old. The branch organization provides all necessary materials such as sheet paper, gummed paper, glue, scissors, patterns, cellophane, candles, bamboo strips and an instruction for making lanterns. The classes are well received by local people, and the seats are always fully booked. The teachers also encourage the learners to take their own lanterns to competitions.

On the afternoon of the Lantern Festival, branch members decorate the trees with colored lights, Chinese knots and festival lanterns, prepare lanterns and candles for sale, and exhibit books on China. Many residents in Canberra community arrive at the meeting place. At the beginning, the host gives a brief introduction to the origin of the Lantern Festival and China's ambassador to Australia makes a speech. Then comes the wonderful performances. When night falls, color lights and lanterns in the tree become the center of attention. A lantern parade, led by two lion dancers, is marching ahead on a small path through a forest near the lake. Over 500 people are involved in it, each holding a lantern in hand.

2. The Lantern Festival in South Korea

In South Korea, the 15th day of the first lunar month is called Yuan Xi Festival. They don't call it the Lantern Festival; instead they just call it the First Full Moon Day.

On this day, Koreans will eat five-cereal meal, nuts, dry

vegetables, and drink Ear-Cleaning Wine. The five-cereal meal consists of glutinous rice, sorghum rice, small red beans, millet, black soya beans. The meal is not easy to cook. Traditionally people use stone pots, but now with the development of technology and lifestyle, electric pressure cooker is preferred. Similar to Chinese rice porridge eaten on the 8th day of the 12th lunar month, the five-cereal meal is not strictly limited to the five cereals. The meal on the day has two meanings: the first is to supplement nutrition in winter, and the second is to express a wish for health and harvest in the new year. Dry vegetables are made of preserved eggplant, pumpkin, radish and wild herbs. It is believed that the dry vegetables may reduce the possibility of heatstroke in the summer of the year. All kinds of nuts, like peanuts, walnuts, pine nuts, chestnuts, may firm up the teeth, and prevent skin diseases. If one drinks the Ear-Cleaning Wine on the morning of the festival, one will hear good news all year round, and will not get ear diseases. The ears will also become more sensitive. The Korean wine is made from pure rice, sending off

Burning the Moon-Room in South Korea

pleasant smell, tasting particularly satisfying.

On the festival in South Korea, varied praying and folk customs are held. One important activity is Burning the Moon Room. In the countryside, villagers get together to put up a cone-shaped room structure with tree trunk or bamboo, cover it up with pine branches and straw, and hang up paper slips of New Year wishes. This is the Moon Room. After the moon rises up in the sky, people will burn down the room, sing and dance near the campfire. The noise of burning trees and bamboos is believed to drive evil spirits. The bigger the fire is, the more prosperous the year becomes. It is an ill omen to have fire extinguished halfway. Besides, people hold many other celebrations, such as kites-flying, tug-of-war, and bridge-crossing, to pray for blessings and prevent from diseases and disasters. On the 15th day of the first lunar month, the festival celebration is also held in many other places in South Korea, such as Chuncheon City, Samchok City, and Jeju Island, which adds exotic flavors to the Lantern Festival.

3. The Lantern Festival in Malaysia

The Lantern Festival is one of the most important traditional festivals among the Chinese Malaysians. The most distinct custom is Tossing Oranges and Bananas.

This custom has a origin in China. In the past, girls seldom stepped out of their houses, and only on the Lantern Festival could they be permitted by parents to go out and watch the festival lanterns. Many young men and women just took this opportunity to look for their beloved. However, when this custom was brought to Malaysia, it became the Tossing of Oranges and Bananas. At the beginning some unmarried girls with Fujian origin believed that a good toss of orange would be rewarded with a good husband. Now, this festival has become a social day for young people. They toss fruits to the sea, the lakes or the ponds at the festival night. Men toss bananas, and girls toss oranges. All the fruits are written a telephone number that is hoped to start a good marriage. Many single people take part in it. Such a custom is still kept in many places like Kuala Lumpur, Kuala Selangor, Penang, and Malacca. Young people in Kuala Lumpur may sit in a circle around a fountain pool. When the fruits are thrown into the water, men will drag for the oranges, while girls will catch the bananas. In Perak, Chinese mass organizations will hold an activity "Romance of Orange" at Guanyin Cave, Ipoh. Young people tie up one's own photo to an orange with a red line, and hang it up on a wish tree, hoping to meet Mr. or Mrs. Right.

The tossing fruits activity has been held near the fountain pool at the Queens Park in Kuala Lumpur for 12 years. A special pool is set up for this custom. In addition, people also have other celebrations such as water lanterns, and praying

Tossing of Oranges and Bananas

235

blessings. The Sunway Lagoon Theme Park has undertaken many fruits-tossing activities and has received great welcome from the public. The necessary items for the activity can be self prepared, or purchased in the park, such as oranges, wish balls, wish paper and some pocket foods. In Penang, the festival celebration is usually held at the sea dike of Fort Cornwallis. On Malacca River, passengers on a pleasure boat may get an orange for free, and write down their wishes or blessings on the orange. After that, they can toss the orange into a designated spot in the river. Single young people may write down their telephone numbers for a possible encounter.

4. The Lantern Festival in Japan

In Japan, the 15th day of the first lunar month is called the Small Festival in the First Lunar Month, and the Spring Festival is the Big Festival in the First Lunar Month. Japanese people don't eat sweet rice balls but red bean porridge to remove ill

The Lantern Fair in Nagasaki, Japan

fortune and disaster. In some rural areas, almost every family will cook a big pot of red bean porridge on the festival. Actually, the red bean porridge in origin was also introduced to Japan from China.

After the Tang Dynasty, in silkworm production area south of Yangtze River, the porridge was gradually replaced by a cocoon-shaped *Yuanxiao* or sweet rice balls, a glutinous rice food. The porridge custom disappeared in China, but it has been kept as a tradition in Japan, being part of the festival celebration with good wishes.

On the 15th day of the first lunar month, all the China Towns in Japan are in celebration of the Lantern Festival. Especially the lantern fair in the Yokohama China Town attracts many local Chinese every year; the whole street is decorated with beautiful lights and colors. The lantern fair begins in the evening, and some other performances are put on at the same time, such as dragon dance, lion dance and classical dance. The splendid programs and festival joy also attract some Japanese people to watch and appreciate.

"元宵"的制作方法

The Recipe of *yuanxiao*

正月十五全家人团团圆圆一起围坐吃元宵、汤圆，是中国春节里的传统时刻。同样白白胖胖的小团子，因地域的差异，叫法与制法却不尽相同。北方叫作元宵，是将糖馅放入笸箩中不断滚摇，用类似滚雪球的方式，使糯米粉逐渐包裹在糖馅外制作而成。南方叫作汤圆，则是用上好的精致糯米粉和成面团，再揉捏入馅料的方法制作而成。

It is a tradition for Chinese people to get together with their families to eat yuanxiao on the Lantern Festival. The white sweet balls have different names and ways of making in different places. In the north people usually roll the sweet balls with a bamboo basket so as to have the sugar fillings wrapped by glutinous flour. While in the south, people name it tangyuan. They knead refined glutinous rice flour into a dough, and add fillings into it.

原材料:
猪板油 120g、黑芝麻 100g、绵白糖
100g、汤圆粉 400g
Ingredients: 120g pork suet, 100g black
sesame seeds,100g soft white sugar,
400g glutinous rice flour

制作步骤 / Procedures

1. 制元宵馅。
取黑芝麻放入平底锅中,用小火耐心翻炒,待听到锅中的黑芝麻发出"啪啪"
声,且能闻到明显的芝麻清香时,黑芝麻就算炒好了。
Stir-fry the black sesame seeds in a saucepan until you smell its fragrance and hear the
cracks.

2. 将黑芝麻倒在案板上摊开，再稍稍放凉，接着用擀面杖擀压成黑芝麻碎，或放入打碎机中搅打成黑芝麻碎。
Pour the sesame seeds onto the chopping board. When they get cooler, smash them into pieces or powder with a rolling pin or a masher.

3. 猪板油切成小丁，把黑芝麻碎、猪板油小丁和绵白糖放入大碗中，用手不断地搅拌抓攥，使 3 种馅料充分糅和在一起，形成一整块，看不到白色的猪板油即可。
Cut the pork suet into slices. Fully mix the sesame powder, pork suet and sugar in a bowl until you cannot see the white pork suet.

4. 将黑芝麻馅料用手均分成若干份，每份约 10g 重，再用手搓成小圆球。
Divide the fillings into several portions, each 10 grams. Rub with hands each portion of fillings into a ball.

附

录

5. 在400g 汤圆粉中逐渐调入250ml 温开水，并用手不停混合搅拌。最后和成一个软硬适中的面团，再静置30分钟，接着将面团搓成长条状，再切成大小均匀的小段。

Place the glutinous rice flour in a large mixing bowl. Add the water, a small amount at a time, all together about 250 milliliters. Shape the dough until it is not too soft, but smooth and easy to manipulate. Wait for another 30 minutes. Rub the dough into the form of a bar, and cut it into average small sections.

6. 用手将粉团搓成圆球状。保持双手的干爽，将粉团放入手中，小心地捏成酒盅状汤圆皮。在每个汤圆皮中放入1枚黑芝麻馅料块，再将面皮边缘向上端收起，直至将黑芝麻馅料块完全包裹住。

Roll the dough into a ball. Keep your hands dry and use your thumb to make a deep indentation in the dough, and place a sesame ball into the hole before closing it up. Make sure the sesame ball is completely covered with the dough.

7. 再将粉团搓和成圆球状，制成汤圆生坯。

Roll the dough again into the shape of a ball.

8.汤锅中放入适量清水,大火烧沸后放入汤圆生坯。用汤勺沿锅边推转,大火煮制约3分钟,待汤圆逐渐浮起。汤水沸腾时,再倒入少许冷水,继续用大火煮制3分钟,最后待汤圆再次全部浮起。最后汤水烧沸后,将汤圆及汤一起盛入碗中即可。

Cook the sweet balls in boiled water. Make sure to keep stirring for 3 minutes in one direction while cooking. When they begin to float on the water, you can add small amount of cold water until it boils again. When the balls float again, it's time to reduce the heat and enjoy the food.

丛书后记

上下五千年的悠久历史孕育了灿烂辉煌的中华文化。我国地域辽阔，民族众多，节庆活动丰富多彩，而如此众多的节庆活动就是一座座珍贵丰富的旅游资源宝藏。在中华民族漫长的历史长河中，春节、清明、端午、中秋等传统节日和少数民族节日，是中华民族优秀传统文化的历史积淀，是中华民族精神和情感传承的重要载体，是维系祖国统一、民族团结、文化认同、社会和谐的精神纽带，是中华民族生生不息的不竭动力。

春节以正月为岁首，贴门神、朝贺礼；元宵节张灯、观灯；清明节扫墓、踏青、郊游、赏牡丹；端午节赛龙舟、包粽子；上巳节祓禊；七夕节乞巧，牛郎会织女；中秋节赏月、食月饼；节日间的皮影戏、长安鼓乐；少数民族的节日赶圩、歌舞美食……这一桩桩有趣的节日习俗，是联络华人、华侨亲情、乡情、民族情的纽带，是中国非物质文化遗产的"活化石"。

为了传播中华民族优秀传统文化，推进中外文化交流，中国人类学民族学研究会民族节庆专业委员会与安徽人民出版社合作，继成功出版《中国节庆文化》丛书之后，再次推出《多彩中国节》丛书。为此，民族节庆专委会专门成立了编纂委员会，邀请了国际节庆协会（IFEA）主席兼首席执行官史迈德·施迈德先生、中国文联原执行副主席冯骥才先生、第十一届全国政协民族和宗教委员会副主任周明甫先生等担任顾问，由《中外节庆网》总编辑彭新良博士担任主编，16位知名学者组成编委会，负责丛书的组织策划、选题确定、体例拟定和作者的甄选。

出版《多彩中国节》丛书，是民族节庆专业委员会和安徽人民出版社合作的结晶。安徽人民出版社是安徽省最早的出版社，有60余年的建社历史，在对外传播方面走在全国出版社的前列；民族节庆专业委员会是我国节庆研究领域唯一的国家级社团，拥有丰富的专家资源和地方节庆资源。这套丛书的出版，实现了双方优势资源的整合。丛书的面世，若能对推动中国文化的对外传播、促进传统民族文化的传承与保护、展示中华民族的文化魅力、塑造节庆的品牌与形象有所裨益，我们将甚感欣慰。

掩卷沉思，这套丛书凝聚着诸位作者的智慧，倾注着编纂者的心血，也诠释着中华民族文化的灿烂与辉煌。在此，真诚感谢各位编委会成员、丛书作者、译者以及出版社工作人员付出的辛劳，以及各界朋友对丛书编纂工作的鼎力支持！希望各位读者对丛书多提宝贵意见，以便我们进一步完善后续作品，将更加璀璨的节庆文化呈现在世界面前。

为了向中外读者更加形象地展示各民族的节庆文化，本丛书选用了大量图片。这些图片，既有来自于丛书作者的亲自拍摄，也有的来自于民族节庆专委会图片库（由各地方节庆组织、节庆主办单位报送并授权使用），还有部分图片是由编委会从专业图片库购买，或从新闻媒体中转载。由于时间关系，无法与原作者一一取得联系，请有关作者与本书编委会联系（邮箱：pxl@jieqing365.com），我们将按相关规定支付稿酬。特此致谢。

《多彩中国节》丛书编委会

2018年3月

Series Postscript

China has developed its splendid and profound culture during its long history of 5000 years. It has a vast territory, numerous nationalities as well as the colorful festivals. The rich festival activities have become the invaluable tourism resources. The traditional festivals, such as the Spring Festival, the Tomb-Sweeping Festival, the Dragon Boat Festival, the Mid-Autumn Festival as well as the festivals of ethnic minorities, represent the excellent traditional culture of China and have become an important carrier bearing the spirits and emotions of Chinese people, a spirit tie for the national reunification, national unity, cultural identity and social harmony, and an inexhaustible motive force for the development of Chinese nation.

The Spring Festival starts with Chinese lunar January, when people post pictures of the Door Gods and exchange gifts and wishes cheerfully. At the Lantern Festival a splendid light show is to be held and enjoyed. On the Tomb-Sweeping Festival, men and women will worship their ancestors by sweeping the tombs, going for a walk in the country and watching the peony. And then the Dragon Boat Festival witnesses a wonderful boat race and the making of zongzi. Equally interesting is the needling celebration on the Double Seventh Festival related to a touching love story of a cowboy and his fairy bride. While the Mid-Autumn Festival is characterized by moon-cake eating and moon watching. Besides all these, people can also enjoy shadow puppet shows, Chang'an drum performance, along with celebration fairs, songs and dances and delicious snacks for ethic groups. A variety of festival entertainment and celebrations have formed a bond among all Chinese, at home or abroad, and they are regarded as the "living fossil" of Chinese intangible cultural heritage.

In order to spread the excellent traditional culture of China, and promote the folk festival brand for our country, the Folk Festival Commission of the China Union of Anthropological and Ethnological Science (CUAES) has worked with the Anhui People's Publishing House to publish *The Colorful Chinese Festivals Series*. For this purpose, the Folk Festival Commission has established the editorial board of *The Colorful Chinese Festivals Series*, by inviting Mr. Steven Wood Schmader, president and CEO of the International Festival And Events Association (IFEA); Mr. Feng Jicai, former executive vice-president of China Federation of Literary and Art Circles(CFLAC); Mr. Zhou Mingfu, deputy director of the Eleventh National and Religious Committee of the CPPCC as consultants; Dr. Peng Xinliang, editor-in-chief of the Chinese and foreign Festival Website as the chief editor; and 16 famous scholars as the members to organize, plan, select and determine the topics and the authors.

This series is the product of the cooperation between the Folk Festival Commission and Anhui People's Publishing House. Anhui People's Publishing House is the first publishing house in Anhui Province, which has a history of over 60 years, and has been in the leading position in terms of foreign transmission. The Folk Festival Commission is the only organization of national level in the field of research of the Chinese festivals, which has experts and rich local festival resources. The series has integrated the advantageous resources of both parties. We will be delighted and gratified to see that the series could promote the foreign transmission of the Chinese culture, promote the inheritance and preservation of the traditional and folk cultures, express the cultural charms of China and build the festival brand and image of China.

The Colorful Chinese Festivals Series is bearing the wisdoms and knowledge of all of its authors and the great efforts of the editors, and explaining the splendid cultures of the Chinese nation. We hereby sincerely express our gratitude to the members of the board, the authors, the translators and the personnel in the publishing house for their great efforts and to all friends from all walks of the society for their supports. We hope you can provide your invaluable opinions for us to further promote the following works so as to show the world our excellent festival culture.

This series uses a large number of pictures in order to unfold the festive cultures in a vivid way to readers at home and abroad. Some of them are shot by the authors themselves, some of them come from the picture database of the Folk Festival Commission (contributed and authorized by the local folk festival organizations or organizers of local festival celebrations), and some of them are bought from Saitu Website or taken from the news media. Because of the limit of time, we can't contact the contributors one by one. Please don't hesitate about contacting the editorial board of this series (e-mail: pxl@ jieqing365.com) if you're the contributor. We'll pay you by conforming to the state stipulations.

Editorial Committee of *The Colorful Chinese Festivals Series*
March, 2018